Commercial Real Estate Investment For Beginners

Faye Belle

Copyright © 2021

All rights reserved to Bohnke Publishing.

No part of this book may be reproduced by any means whatsoever without the written permission of the author, except for very brief portions of the book which may be quoted for the purpose of review.

Table of contents

Introduction 7

Chapter 1 12

  Just What Is Commercial Real Estate? 12

    Commercial Real Estate Defined 12

    Investment versus Use 13

    Comfort Zone 14

    Setting Realistic Goals 15

Chapter 2 20

  Why Commercial Real Estate Is A Dynamic Investment 20

    Invested Amount = Cash + Debt + Time 21

    Other People's Money 21

    Leveraged Cash Flow 23

    Equity Buildup 26

    Appreciation You Can Accelerate 26

    Management Postures 1, 2, 3, and 4 28

    Supply and Demand 31

    The Seven Dynamics of Commercial Real Estate 32

    How Not to Be Intimidated by Commercial Real Estate . 44

    The Four Real Estate Myths That Need to Be Unveiled .. 46

Chapter 3 57

  What Makes Real Estate Value Go Up or Down 57

    Key Words and Concepts to Build Your Insider Knowledge 59

    Six Primary Factors That Make Real Estate Value Go Up or Down . 77

Chapter 4 101

How to Build an Effective Commercial Real Estate Comfort Zone 101
    Concepts to Build Your Insider Knowledge 102
    Listing Service 102
    FSBO 103
    Active Listings 103
    Tax Assessor 104
    MapQuest 105
    Zoning Maps 106
    Elements Common to All Initial Comfort Zones 109
    Key Factors to Becoming an Expert in Your Own Backyard 113
    Learn How to Let Your Computer Lead the Way to Your Success 120
    How to Choose Your Comfort Zone 122

Chapter 5 133
  How to Accomplish Effective Due Diligence 133
    Key Words and Concepts to Build Your Insider Knowledge 136
    Due Diligence by Definition 137
    The Eight Most Important Elements of Due Diligence 152
    The Four Elements to Prepare for Due Diligence 168
    Eight Things You Can Do When You Find Problems 172
  Conclusion 181

Introduction

If you think commercial real estate is just like residential real estate except that you need more capital to get started, you are in for a surprise. Commercial real estate is completely different and often requires little or no capital, there are so many opportunities for creativity, thinking outside of the box, and coming up with wacky ideas, it genuinely is a lot of fun.

Please also bear in mind that this is based on my experience in the field and it should **not** be taken as financial advice. This book is purely informative and aims to close knowledge gaps in this area so that you are better prepared to make wise decisions.

Residential real estate truly is, in my opinion, a much better investment than stocks, bonds, mutual funds, Treasury bills, certificates of deposit, commodities, options, futures, and unit trusts, for certain reasons. However, when faced with a choice between residential and commercial real estate, I would recommend commercial real estate as your way to riches. Certainly, with my own investing, I have long ago focused almost exclusively on commercial properties, for reasons that I share in this book.

Many people think commercial real estate is too complex, too specialized, too esoteric, and too difficult for you to even consider, then let me take you on a journey to convince you that it is none of these things. In fact, I firmly believe that after reading this book, you will no longer want to even consider residential real estate as an investment option, and will focus instead on commercial real estate with both enthusiasm and confidence. The only regret you may have is that you didn't discover this information sooner.

Consider this: of all the wealthy ($100 million plus net worth) property investors I have come across, at most two have made their fortune through residential property, the rest have all done it through commercial property.

Think about this, you wouldn't choose a surgeon with a low patient survival rate when there are others with a high survival rate. You wouldn't choose a car with a low crashtest rating over one with a high rating, or a school for your kids with a low graduation rate over one with a high graduation rate. So now that you know that nearly all wealthy property investors have achieved their wealth through commercial real estate, how can you justify even thinking of buying one more residential property?

It would be like dropping your kids off at a bad school, and driving yourself in an unsafe car to a hospital to have surgery performed on you by a surgeon with a low patient survival rate. That is nuts, right? Well, in relative terms, so is investing in residential real estate.

This book is designed for whatever level of real estate expertise the reader may have, and is neither condescending nor complicated. It is a building block of tried and true steps designed to let any investor succeed in commercial real estate at his or her own pace.

Each chapter begins with a description of its principal goals. To help you stay on track, each chapter also lists key words and concepts, which are then discussed in some detail. While these elements pertain mainly to the goals of the chapter, they also introduce insider secrets and other concepts and tech niques that will be important tools as you begin to implement the interim steps which will lead you to success later on.

You will get the maximum benefit from this book if you begin to implement the steps as you read about them. The majority of the tasks you will be asked to do are designed to turn you into a real estate insider. As you begin to learn the real insider secrets from the book, and build your real estate vocabulary of words and concepts, you will also see how easy it is to rub elbows with other real estate insiders. If there is any doubt as to who they are, don't worry. I not only tell you how to find them, but I give you tips on how to get the most out of your new sphere of friends and future business associates.

What this book is not: This book is not heavy theory with what if examples that are unrealistic and difficult to follow. There are no complex mathematical and analytical processes such as are found in many real estate books today. That kind of investing often loses more great deals for the investor than it produces. Besides the key to success in any kind of real estate is to know your local market, and to build your own comfort zone.This simple factor will be your springboard to success.

☐

Chapter 1
Just What Is Commercial Real Estate?

Goal: How to get started in commercial real estate

key words:

Commercial Real Estate Defined

Investment vs Use

Comfort Zone

Setting Realistic Goals

Commercial Real Estate Defined

For the purpose of this book, commercial real estate is considered to be any real estate that has the ability to produce outside revenue or income for you as an investor in that property. This can include a vacant lot or tract of land on which you intend to construct a building to rent out, or land that can itself be leased to a user and thereby produce income. A duplex or apartment building in which you live while you rent out the other units is considered a commercial property. A single family home where you live is not, at that moment, a commercial property. If you later make changes to the property such that you can generate income, whether or not you still live there, then the property becomes a form of commercial property.

Investment versus Use
It is essential to distinguish between the two elements of investment and use. Let's start with an investment property. When you find a property you wish to invest in, it is a property that you anticipate will return a profit to you at a future date. A property you intend to use may end up being a good investment, but your original goal is not to profit directly from the real estate but, rather, to profit from your personal use of it. You might need an office to house your business, so you buy one to use. Or you may need a home and, rather than rent, you buy one to use. The concept of use is important, because it includes other factors that make a property valuable for more reasons than just profit from income or a future sale.

This book delves deeply into the different reasons people buy real estate. To set the stage, consider that a person buys a home or apartment near a great school or work or medical care for reasons oriented to those services, and not solely for future profit. Grasp the idea that use may be the ultimate deciding factor in the purchase of a property, and that it may even be the sole reason for its value to a specific user. Keep in mind right from the start, not all properties can be used for every possible use. By the time you have completed this book you will understand that the key insider secret to investing in commercial real estate is use, and in the long run use governs profit.

Comfort Zone

I use the term comfort zone to refer to the investment area that you establish. It will begin as a small part of your neighborhood or other area of town, perhaps where you work. Your long range goal is to become an expert in everything that goes on, from a real estate and value point of view, within that comfort zone. You will slowly expand the zone until it contains more of the kind of properties which you might eventually want to own. Your task is to become comfortable in every way with the kind of real estate you are going to buy. For example, if you want to own small apartment buildings, you will define the area of town where you will become knowledgeable of what is going on in the apartment rental business in that area as well as in adjoining areas that may also affect your area.

Setting Realistic Goals

I have already mentioned the importance of goals. To reinforce the earlier statement: A worthy goal is one that is realistic to your abilities, is task oriented, is measurable, has a timetable attached to it, and has merit or worth other than simply the dollar sign at its end. It is easy to say, "My goal is to have ten million dollars" and truly want that to happen. But that kind of goal generally brings you only disappointment. The missing ingredients are those other elements.

■ Goals should be realistic to your abilities. First of all, what are your abilities? By this I don't mean the list of things you are capable of doing right now. You need to include those talents that you can unleash or expand. A class in general contracting or in decorating might be a good start, if that is something you have a good feel for. "Realistic to your abilities" would not mean becoming an airline pilot, for example, unless you have the time to learn how to fly, get the needed experience to be hired by an airline, and enjoy flying in the first place.

■ The goal must be task oriented. This means you have to do something to make the goal come about. Sitting on your duff waiting for the lotto number you picked to come up is not exactly a task oriented event. "I will become an expert in my comfort zone" is a good goal only if you then go out and do what is necessary to become that expert. Good news on that front: I can show you exactly what you will need to do, and the rest will be up to you. Becoming an expert in your comfort zone is exactly what one of your primary goals will be. You might as well write that one down right now. Everything this book points to is how to obtain that status, then how to use the status and your newfound knowledge to reach your financial targets.

■ The goal must be measurable. The goal to be rich is one you will likely never reach, because most rich people I know are driven by the dollar sign and never feel they are rich enough. So, by measurable, I'm not talking about the concept of being rich, but an obtainable amount of money. To do this, first think of the end result: say, to become financially independent. As you move toward that long range goal, check on your progress from time to time. How far along are you in reaching that point? A good measuring point might be to set, as the goal you first target, the amount of money you are currently earning from your present job. Write down your present wages and then aim to obtain that amount over and above what you earn from your current job from your real estate investments.

■ The goal must have a timetable tied to it. If you have carefully followed the idea of a realistic goal, then you should have some idea of how long it might take to get there. If you set a deadline of two years to own your own home, and a year goes by and you have not even been out looking for homes or haven't even picked a neighborhood you would like to live in, I'd say you need to reevaluate your timetable. It might be that you underestimated the steps you need to accomplish before you know enough to achieve the goal. It's okay to change your goal once you have set it up, timetable and all, but don't wait two years to do that. And when you do make a change, be sure you understand the reason for making it.

■ The goal must have merit or worth beyond a dollar amount. Ask this question of yourself: "Why do I want to own several small apartment buildings?" The right answer is not "to become a millionaire." The answer should fit into a longer range plan. A longer range plan is, in essence, a goal on a bigger scale. All goals should be structured so that short range goals are designed to be steps up the ladder. As you achieve them, you are moving in the direction of the longer range goal.

Far too many people set long range goals but then fail to grasp that while their goal: for instance, to move to Paris might be okay, there is something missing. For example, how do you get to the point that you will be able to support yourself (and family) once you got there? Or, perhaps, what do you do to obtain sufficient funds to be so financially independent that you will be able to retire? Each element that leads you toward your long range goal is in itself nothing more than an achieved segment on a road map to your desired destination.

Whether real estate is to be a part of the destination or only a step that takes you there, this book will allow you to develop a plan that will help you achieve your goal. Once you are on your way and begin to move up the ladder of attainment of goals, you can keep raising your sights. Start with the smallest elements possible until you discover that all the goals you set, you attain. How about this as your next goal: "I will read this book within the next 20 days." Then go on to, "I will start to follow the steps to develop a comfort zone and become a real estate insider."

The next chapter of this book will begin your formation or reformation, as the case may be into a highly effective and successful real estate investor.

Chapter 2
Why Commercial Real Estate Is A Dynamic Investment

Goals:

To Introduce You to the World of Commercial Real Estate.

To Illustrate the Ease in Building Financial Independence with Commercial Real Estate.

Key Words and Concepts to Build Your Insider Knowledge.

Invested Amount = Cash + Debt + Time

Other People's Money

Leveraged Cash Flow

Equity Buildup

Appreciation You Can Accelerate

Management Postures 1, 2, 3 and 4

Supply & Demand.

Invested Amount = Cash + Debt + Time
The real cost of every real estate investment can be broken down to this simple equation. The amount of your investment is ultimately the total of the cash you invest, the debt you take on, and the value of the time you spend. Each of these elements has its importance, and the degree of importance differs relative to each investor's circumstance. If you have a lot of free cash, then the debt and time you spend may be reduced. It can go the other way too: If you are short of cash and have to max out your mortgage and other debt potentials, then you might have to spend a lot more time to turn the investment into a real winner.
Nowhere in this equation should you consider that the invested amount is the same as what you paid for the property, without including your time as a part of that overall value. It is okay for you to discount the value of your time to a certain degree, as being your own boss has its own real value. But do put a value to your time.

Other People's Money
Other people's money is a factor available to the real estate investor that simply is not a realistic option to an investor in any other commodity. Sure, you can buy stocks on a

margin account, or commodities like pork bellies and gold at a fraction of what they sell for, but those items won't give you rental income. And if your margin is called and you don't have cash or credit to meet the shortage, then you can get wiped out overnight.

Real estate is where it is at, and other people's money (or just OPM for short) is the name of that game. OPM comes in many forms. It is the money you borrow from the local savings and loan association when you buy your home, or the loan you get from FHA on a four unit apartment building, or the loan from an insurance company for a shopping center you want to build. It can come from many other sources, including a second mortgage from the seller, or your brother-in-law, or a guy you know who hangs around your local pub. It is all money that either you have to pay back or get when you give up a piece of the action. In the case of using OPM to buy your home, it is money that you owe for which you make payments every month. Those payments come out of your pocket and, while it is better than paying rent, it is still a reduction from the amount of money you have in your pocket. When you use OPM in investing in commercial real estate, you are able to double dip at the

OPM wells. This means simply that you dip into the lender's well, and then you dip into your tenant's well when you pay back the lender. Many examples used in this book demonstrate how important OPM is in all kinds of real estate investing. Your maximum benefit from using this book will come through your ability to become as comfortable as you can with as many OPM techniques as possible.

Leveraged Cash Flow

A lever is used to pry up something. In commercial real estate investing, you use OPM as a lever to increase the yield (rate of return) on your investments. You obtain leveraged cash flow when you obtain OPM at a lower cost than the return you are getting from your investments. For example, if you are able to invest $100,000 in an apartment building that gives you a cash flow (money left at the end of the year) of $15,000 a year, after all operational expenses (excluding possible income taxes), you have just received 15 percent on the invested $100,000. However, if you invest only $20,000 in cash and borrow $80,000 of OPM at an annual cost of $7,000, and all other expenses remain the same, then you end up with $8,000 clear. As your cash investment is only $20,000 and the cash in your pocket is $8,000, that is a 40 percent return. The increase from 15 percent to 40 percent is the leverage you have obtained. Expenses to own and operate real estate vary depending on the type of property, the level of maintenance and upgrades you give to that property, and the cost of real estate tax and insurance. Other minor expenses include management and other professional fees. The greatest variables from place to place will be real estate tax, insurance, and utilities. If you can handle the management part yourself, and an occasional weekend with a paint brush to handle the maintenance and upgrade part, it will mean more cash in your pocket. Take a look at these numbers:

Purchase price of the property $100,000

Other people's money (mortgage) 80,000

Cash you invest 20,000

Annual cash flow in this example 15,000

(Prior to Mortgage Payment)

Debt service 7,000

(Your Mortgage Payment)

Cash flow (in your pocket) $8,000

Return on your cash invested 40 percent

Note: Your annual income is still $15,000. Deducting the $7,000 you pay for the

$80,000 loan leaves you with $8,000, which is 40 percent of the $20,000 you invested. The key is getting OPM at a lower cost than your return.

On the other hand, if the cost of the $80,000 was $14,000, you would be left with only

$1,000 at the end of the year ($15,000–$14,000 = $1,000), and that is only a 5 percent return on your invested $20,000. You have not leveraged your return at all. Is this all bad? That depends. If the only way you could buy this property was to finance the $80,000 at that higher cost, and you ended up with an apartment building in which you could improve the rental income to your favor, then you might be able to build the income to $20,000 or more and still come out like a bandit. Besides, as you will discover before finishing this chapter, even if you eventually sold the apartment building for less than $100,000 you might still profit very nicely indeed.

Equity Buildup

As you pay off a mortgage or any other debt, you may be increasing your equity. I say "may be" because if you are letting the property go into disrepair at the same time, it may drop in value faster than you are paying off the debt. But, with prudent investing, you should be able to increase rents and have the benefit of appreciation, as well as pay off a mortgage. Even if the property value does not go up one cent, by the time you pay off that $80,000 debt on the apartment house, you have an equity buildup of $80,000. Remember, you invested only $20,000 and double dipped by having tenants pay off the $80,000 for you.

Appreciation You Can Accelerate

Appreciation refers to the increase in the value of a property over a period of time. The reasons that property values go up are the principal subject of Chapter 3, so I won't spend much time on them at this juncture. The key element here is the fact that there are things you can do to increase the amount of appreciation over a set period of time.

Consider two identical apartment buildings across the street from each other. Even though these two buildings are in the same immediate area, they might be in different cities. Boundary lines between cities and even counties generally run down the center of a street. The very fact that one property is in a different city than the other can greatly affect it's value. Why? Zoning, setbacks, and other local building rules may differ. The flexibility of ultimate use may also vary. For example, one building may sit on a lot that is zoned to allow professional offices, whereas the other, directly across the street, can only be used for residential apartments. This fact alone may have a profound effect 10 years from now when professional offices are better suited for the street, which by then has become a major traffic artery in town and too noisy for high priced apartment rentals. The savvy investor would have checked these factors out prior to buying and, by recognizing the future advantage of a broader use zoning, would have made the moves to quickly take advantage of a higher economic return from professional offices if the trend goes that way.

One of the best ways to accelerate the appreciation is to let nature do it for you. Well landscaped commercial properties can take on a mature value that the barren parking lot of a similar property never achieves. But remember, landscaping is something that most communities are very particular about, so do not jump in and plant trees that may not be approved by the city. Sit down with the appropriate person in the city and get a list of what is allowed, and what they think would be the best plant for the intended area. Keep in mind that some plants tend to drop nasty things on cars parked under them, or millions of leaves each fall, and hard round things, like coconuts, that can damage property as well as people.

One of the most prudent ways to accelerate appreciation is through the right kind of management for the specific property.

Management Postures 1, 2, 3, and 4
Each owner has the choice to do one of the following forms of management. Let's call them management postures 1, 2, 3, and 4. I refer to these management postures periodically throughout this book, so you may want to mark this page for easy reference.

Management posture 1: Do nothing to maintain the property.

Management posture 2: Do very little to maintain the property unless it is actually broken.

Management posture 3: Maintain the property in its original condition.

Management posture 4: Maintain the property in a constant upgrade mode.

It should be obvious that if the property has the potential for a long economic life, management posture (MP) 4 is the least expensive in the long run because the value of the property goes up faster than with MP 1, 2, or 3. There is no single reason for this, but one important lesson to learn is that investors who constantly strive to upgrade their properties are able to increase rent and, in the long run, reduce the percentage of gross income that is spent on maintenance.

How so? Assume your property grosses $100,000 in rents, and after all expenses and debt service you have a cash flow of $15,000. Assume also that all other expenses remain the same, except you increase your maintenance by $2,000. If you spent 6 percent of your gross rents on maintenance last year, or $6,000, and you increase that sum to

$8,000, and the improved condition of the property allows you to bring in a new gross rent of $105,000, your cash flow has jumped up to $18,000 for the year. That $2,000 added cost brought you in an additional $3,000 in revenue. But more important, if an investor wanted 10 percent return on his or her investment, it increased the value of the property by $30,000.

Last year's gross rent $100,000

Less all expenses and debt payments 85,000

Cash flow in your pocket $ 15,000

Next year's gross rent $105,000

Less all expenses 87,000

New cash flow $ 18,000

Added value $ 30,000

This occurs because an additional price of $30,000 will be justified because of the added $3,000 of cash flow.

Chapter 3 introduces the Rule of Small, which should open your eyes to how important your management posture is to your overall value.

Supply and Demand

The interplay between supply and demand is an economic function that has to do with the level of demand for something and the amount of that "something" that is available. The only open cold drink stand on a busy street in downtown Phoenix in July will make more money than the cold drink stand in Buffalo, New York, in January. By the way, a solitary cold drink stand in the middle of the desert is only valuable if there are people who want (and can afford) cold drinks. When you apply this to real estate, you find that you don't have to start out today with what will be in greater demand five years from now, all you have to do is end up with it.

For example, assume the current trend in an area is the development of new luxury rental apartment buildings. It would be safe to assume that this is because there is a demand for that product now. So you look around the same area and find apartment buildings that are not quite up to the same quality level as the new apartments. This would mean lower cost to buy, and less rent to collect. However, if you buy apartment buildings that are less than luxury rentals now and augment a plan to upgrade the units over a period of about five years, your buildings will continue to stay rented because there will always be tenants who cannot afford the higher priced luxury apartments.

As you implement the management plan (MP 4) to bring your apartments up to a status much higher than you began with, you continually accelerate the appreciation of your property. Five years later your apartments are at the level the luxury rentals started at, and you are easily able to rent your apartments at a small discount over the now five year old luxury apartments.

The Seven Dynamics of Commercial Real Estate

There are seven factors that apply to commercial real estate to a much greater degree than to single family real estate. Let's look at each of these incentives in detail.

1. Ability to produce income

2. High yield through double dipping

3. Job security

4. Tax shelter

5. Easy to Create New Value

6. Inflation Fighter

7. Sell for Less than You Paid and Still Make a Huge Profit

Ability to Produce Income

Commercial real estate will generally produce a higher rental return than single family homes can produce. This statement takes into consideration the fact that if you have one single family home and it is vacant, you have, for that period of time at least, a 100 percent vacancy factor to consider. Single family homes may require a higher maintenance cost than other properties and, in general, the single family home as a rental property does not appreciate as rapidly because of overall wear and tear. A portfolio of 100 single family homes spread all over town would be far more of a management headache than a single complex of 200 rental apartments. The synergy of income potential goes up as you reduce the cost to keep the facility in operation. Remember that fact when you consider single family homes over multifamily housing or other kinds of commercial real estate.

High Yield through Double Dipping

I have already touched on the double dipping effect of getting your OPM for the purchase from one well and the payments to meet your debt obligation from another well. This factor alone can create a great win win situation. Let's say you have $50,000 to invest, and you find a $500,000 commercial building containing seven shops that are all rented. You have negotiated the deal to the point where you are able to obtain financing in the total amount of $450,000. To show you how easy that might be, consider a first mortgage in the amount of $400,000 from a local savings and loan association, and the seller holding the remaining $50,000 which is secured by your mother's oceanfront condo (naturally you get her approval first!). Assume that you use all but $5,000 a year of the income to pay off the debt and are able to do that in 12 years. What do you have?

If you elected to use MP 4, it is likely that in those 12 years the property has increased in value to over $1,000,000. Your equity buildup has been 100 percent, so there is no debt on the property at all. You have received a 10 percent return on your investment for each year of your ownership, which would be a total of $60,000. What if you could only sell the property for $400,000 ($100,000 less than you paid for it)? Well, you would put that $400,000 in your pocket. Not such a bad situation, is it.

Price $500,000

Mortgage   450,000

Cash invested $ 50,000 Price less mortgage (OPM)

Cash Flow $5,000 per year, which is a 10 percent yield.

Cash in your pocket $ 60,000 over 12 years.

Mortgage in 12 years 0

Blowout sale $400,000. $100,000 less than your original purchase price.

Profit $350,000. plus you also get back your original $50,000 invested

Job Security

Many people find that real estate can provide them with the most important benefit of all: job security. Many family businesses are tied to real estate farms, roadside fruit stands, landscaping nurseries, restaurants, motels and hotels, and so on. Often it is the food business that first attracts foreigners who come to the United States with little more than the knowledge of how to cook their own ethnic dishes.

Hunger is a great motivator, and how many such restaurants have you entered where most of the staff are members of the same family? Many more than you might realize. I know of families who have worked their way up the financial ladder of success, building grand fortunes in the motel and hotel business, starting with a small facility and ending up with oceanfront flagship hotels worth millions of dollars. One of the factors that all of these people ultimately learn is that owning their place of business is the best way to go. It is in these family run businesses that all the value producing aspects of real estate can come together. Any business that adopts as its mission statement that it will succeed only by delivering to its customers the best service possible (food, hotel rooms, plants, or whatever) ensures that its own goals will be achieved. As the owners build a business that has value, they also cause the real estate in which it is situated to have increases in value.

Tax Shelter

A tax shelter is another form of OPM. This occurs because the Internal Revenue Service

(IRS) allows investors to deduct operational expenses, which are real dollars spent, from the gross income collected to arrive at the taxable income. The IRS also allows the owner to deduct a "paper entry" amount from the gross revenue for depreciation of the value of the property. You can depreciate 100 percent of an improvement, except for the actual land value, and any salvage value that can be calculated. The amount deducted from the gross revenue that falls into this paper entry category of deduction (depreciation and, in the case of groves and mines, depletion) is like borrowing OPM from the government. As this deduction is a paper entry only, it reflects a decrease in the book value of your property and not an actual cash payout. But best of all, it is taken directly from the bottom line at the end of the year.

This means that if you have $20,000 cash left over after all real expenses (operational expenses for the property, including interest on the mortgage), and then can take another paper entry deduction of $5,000, then you pay tax on $15,000 of income but actually have $20,000. If you do that over 10 years you have put a total of $50,000 in your pocket that you did not pay tax on. The tax bite might have been a total of $10,000 or more, but you don't ever have to pay that to Uncle Sam (or the IRS) unless you sell the property and have a profit above your new tax basis.

Without Depreciation

Rents you collect after paying $20,000 (cash in your pocket) operational expenses.

Tax you might have had to pay 4,000 (at 20 percent rate) on the $20,000.

Cash left over as spendable cash $16,000.

With Depreciation

Rents you collect after paying $20,000 operational expenses.

Depreciation allowed by the IRS 5,000.

The amount you report as $15,000 earnings to the IRS.

The amount you actually got $20,000.

Tax you pay (assume minimum 1,750 (paid on the lower $15,000) of 15 percent).

Spendable cash $18,250.

Additional money in your $22,500 pocket over 10 years.

The tax basis of any improved property is the book value of the property which you have created by lowering the original purchase value by the amount of depreciation taken on its improvements while you owned the property. Tax shelter is less of an issue today because the tax rates have come down over past years and the amount of depreciation taken must be spread out over a longer period of time. However, it is a factor to keep in mind when every penny might count.

Easy to Create New Value

There are many ways to create nearly instant value at a very low cost when it comes to real estate. I have purchased buildings that simply needed to be cleaned up to double my investment. One such example was an office condo where my present office is located. The space I purchased had been trashed by the previous owners when they moved out to larger offices downtown. It was twice the area I needed, but I had done my research on the building and the site and discovered that I could actually split the office into two separate condo units. With a local carpenter/painter doing the work, we installed a new entrance into the main hallway for half of the suite of offices. I then put both units on the market.

My decision was to sell one side of the office (whichever side first sold) and keep the remaining one. For one side, I was able to get a price that was equal to what I had paid for the total area, plus enough to cover almost all of the cleaning, painting, and carpentry needed to turn it into two offices.

Another building I purchased was a very old, wooden, single family home. It had not been painted, inside or out, for 20 years or longer and was a shambles. It was located on a busy business street and had been occupied by a frame shop for the previous 10 years. Many of the rooms were filled with leftover frame stock and simply needed to be emptied, cleaned up, and painted. I offered a local summer camp all the old frame stock if they came and got it (they used it in their summer arts and craft department of the camp). I hired day labor to scrub the place down with TSP (trisodium phosphate is one of the best cleaning compounds you will ever buy, and is found in any hardware store or paint shop) and then pressure clean the results. A painter arrived a few days later and, using a pressure spray machine, gave the inside and out several new coats of white paint. The building sold a week later at a nice profit of twice the price I paid. Landscaping is another great way to create both instant and long improving value. Many older properties suffer from deteriorating landscaping around them or are over grown with plants. Each situation presents different challenges, but the end result can be an instant improvement with the longer term growth of a beautiful yard at a relatively low cost. If you are looking for a longer period of growth (say you are going to use the building for five years yourself) then spend less money by purchasing the kinds and sizes of plants that will reach their greater value in five years. This book gives many such examples of instant or near instant creation of value.

Inflation fighter.

Commercial property is a great inflation fighter because the owner is able to dip, and double dip, into the OPM wells. If you can lock up a large percentage of the original cost of the property in the form of a mortgage or other debt used to purchase the property, at an interest rate that will still allow you to have a positive cash flow (some money left over at the end of the year), then all the inflation in the world will only benefit you. This is what makes real estate such a sweet form of investing.

Sell for Less than You Paid and Still Make a Big Profit.

One of the sweetest aspects of real estate is that through the combination of OPM and a sound investment strategy, you have a built in safety net. This safety net is so good that even if you make a pretty bad mistake, you can come out smelling like a rose.

Here is another example of this magic:

Say you buy a small strip store for a total price of $600,000. You invest a total of $100,000 in up front value (cash and/or exchange of services or property), and the balance of

$500,000 is made up of total debt (first mortgage from a bank and some seller held financing). The terms are set so that you pocket only $7,000 each year after all expenses (which include your accountant and lawyer), but you are also able to pay off the total debt over a 15 years so that at the end of that time you own the property free and clear of debt.

Let's look at two situations. In the first scenario, you made a great investment, and over the years you raise rents to the extent that your total cash earnings for the 15 years is $220,000. This translates to an average cash flow of $14,666.67 per year, a comfortable 14.67 percent annual return on your investment. After a 15 year holding period, the property should have appreciated to at least $1,000,000 in value and is all yours, free and clear. Your cash income for the 16th year should be over $120,000 because you no longer have any debt to pay.

Now let the safety net come into play. Your investment starts out okay, but after the third year your income stays at a lower level. You end up, after 15 years, having earned a cash flow of only $125,000 for the entire time. So you decide to sell, and the best offer you can get is $500,000 after selling costs less than you paid for the property. But wait, you only invested $100,000, and you did earn interest on that at double or more what you could get

the bank. On top of that, you had some tax shelter along the way and are still able to walk away from the closing office with a check for $500,000. That is still a profit of $400,000 over what you started with. Only in real estate can this happen.

A Recap of This Example

Original price of the property

$600,000

Cash invested 100,000

Mortgage (OPM) 500,000

Total cash in your pocket over $125,000 15 years

Ultimate sales price $500,000

Your profit $400,000 plus your $100,000 investment back.

How Not to Be Intimidated by Commercial Real Estate

I frequently give courses on the subject of "Successful Commercial Real Estate Brokerage." There is generally a good turnout of salesmen and saleswomen who come to learn how they can escape the housing market and get into the part of brokerage where the real money is to be found. They leave the program with a new respect for what they thought they needed to escape from, because they recognize that the same fundamentals that work for successful home brokers will also work for real estate firms that specialize in selling large commercial or investment properties.

However, there is one major element that they must overcome. They need to stop being intimidated by the aspect of commercial real estate. Over the years I have discovered that this fear or intimidation extends well beyond the salesmen and saleswomen who deal with this kind of property it also affects the investors who might otherwise seek to buy and invest in commercial properties. I believe this happens because people think that commercial or investment properties require a level of investment savvy or financial education that is greater than they possess or are capable of obtaining. I can assure you that I know many people who have made a great success out of owning strip stores, shopping plazas, office buildings, rental apartments, and other kinds of commercial properties, but who have never graduated from college. Many have worked hard to attain their success, even those who have come to the United States unable to speak English with just a few dollars in their pockets. Why were they not intimidated? My guess is simply because they didn't know they were supposed to be intimidated.

Even so, the aura of complication still hovers and is just one of the many myths that exist about real estate. Once you face them and discover that even many of the real insiders don't know the truth about them, you will be able to face them down and no longer be intimidated about any aspect of the real estate investment arena.

The Four Real Estate Myths That Need to Be Unveiled
Commercial Real Estate Is Complicated

The proponents of this myth will fill their arguments with statements such as "Commercial real estate is filled with heavy and complex math, international finance, reams of forms and applications and reports to be filed, mystifying tax complications, and legal ramifications that can send you to jail if you screw up." Now, as with all myths, it takes some truth to keep the myth alive. There is some math involved, only you don't have to do it. The same is true with forms and taxes and all that. That is what accountants and lawyers are for. They are cheap if you start with them and only expensive if you try to do it yourself and need them to bail you out of a jam. The fact is that the benefits of getting into multitenant investment property far outweigh the complications that you will be able to farm out to hired help. The investor who is trying to make his investment capital work for him by keeping the books, collecting the rents, inspecting the property, and doing the year end tax reporting is doing more than he should be doing. So don't get caught in that trap.

By the time you are halfway into this book, you will understand that knowing what is going on in the marketplace is 90 percent of the effort. Arriving at this level of knowledge is simple, easy, and fun, and does take some time. This is the time that you will devote to making contacts that will work for you year after year and cost you nothing more than the time it took to meet them and to cultivate them as your friends and business associates. It is also the time you will spend getting to know what creates value within your comfort zone, and how you can take advantage of the obvious signals that have been sitting right on the next door neighbor's fence all the time, only you didn't recognize them.

The other 10 percent of the ingredients needed to fill out the formula for success are elements that you will absorb all by yourself as you work your way up the ladder of becoming a true real estate insider. It is to meet these ends that this book is dedicated. As you may suspect, 90 percent of the book is designed to hold your hand and lead you through the initial 90 percent of your effort. Not once will you be asked to take an SAT test, or attend graduate school, or apply to law school. No one will ask to see your diploma.

This book and the lessons it provides will get you started on the right path and propel you as far as your own motivation and ability will carry you. You will be asked to do everything you can to expand your sphere of reference (the people around you and your knowledge of what is going on in your own growing backyard). Is this book the last book you will ever read on the subject? I truly hope not. Not only do I continue to write more books on the subject, but I also am an avid reader of many aspects of this exciting field. I know the necessity to maintain a current posture in the

marketplace, and that requires me (and you too) to become a student of real estate for as long as I hope to be successful in it. Become a sponge and absorb all you can about the subject. But never be intimidated again, never.

Real Estate Is Management Intensive

Remember management postures 1, 2, 3, and 4? They are the foundations to all real estate management you need to begin with. You will add finesse to each of them as you go along. You will discover that MP 4 is not always the best approach to real estate management. Sure, MP 4 is ideal for property you plan to keep for a while, and property that is not already near its economic obsolescence. There are times when you simply want to keep the property producing income, at its highest level, for a short period of time. This means you do not want to plow more capital into a property that is going to be torn down in a few years. In such cases, MP 2 or MP 3 might be all that is needed. You will also discover that the Rule of Small works with almost every aspect of real estate and especially applies to the management side of things. The Rule of Small, which governs the financial mastery of real estate where small moves give big end results, is discussed in detail in Chapter 3.

The most important aspect of real estate management is to deal with it quickly and decisively without big moves. Tenant complaints should be addressed and not ignored, problem tenants removed if possible, and rents kept at or below the market rate of similar properties. If the property is in a constant upgrade program (MP 4), then stay at or above market rates.

The Three Most Important Words Are "Location, Location, Location"

I love to discuss this subject because virtually everyone I come across has it all wrong. The idea of "location, location, location" as the three most important words was coined by an unknown person, or surely by someone too embarrassed to admit to having coined that phrase. I can only suspect that the point this person was trying to make was that where a property is located is the most important aspect of that property. Now, there is a smidgin of truth in this statement. Location does have both merit and value. But as you will shortly understand, it is not the location that makes the property most valuable.

Let's begin by looking at two corners of a very busy intersection in a prosperous city in the

United States. Each corner is exactly the same size, and each street that makes up this intersection is equally important, with the same amount of traffic at all times of the day. All four corners of the intersection have the same advantage as to location, with only very small differences. These differences would apply to the direction of the heaviest traffic at certain times of the day, as at most intersections traffic flow tends to shift to a certain degree; bright sun reflections in morning or afternoon drivers' eyes; and existing buildings that adjoin the corner can influence where a person decides to turn in. But let's ignore those minor elements, as the question at hand is the location only.

These four corners have essentially the same value. But are there other factors we should be looking at? Is location alone enough of a criterion to establish value? No. The most important aspect of any property is the allowed use. This aspect comes in several packages. First, what is the use the buyer intends for that property? This is important because if you are an investor looking to make a great investment, and you believe you have found a great location in town and can buy the remaining corner at half the price that the other three have sold for, that should be all you need to know. Right?

Wrong. As an investor, you may not have a clue what the future use of this property will be. Will it be a fast food facility, a bank, a parking lot, or what? So the word use must be viewed as referring to the possible uses that the local zoning and other restrictions will allow. In essence, what will they let you put there? If you are the actual user looking for a place to put one of your existing businesses say a tire store, or a muffler shop, or a full service restaurant with lounge, your first choice may be to find a good location, but you need a location that allows the use that you need. The best location in the world, if it does not allow a muffler shop, will have no value Muffler stores.

Use, then, is a critical element that needs to be understood. Use is controlled by a number of factors, some governmental in nature, such as zoning ordinances, controls dealing with fire issues, and regulations about hazardous substances (relating to such things as gas storage, paint booths, and chemical sales). Deed restrictions imposed by past owners or developers can also restrict use, as can setbacks from other similar uses or prohibitions on activities within so many feet of their front door. Use is the key to the value of any location.

The subject of use and all the elements that control it is discussed in the balance of this book. It will be very important for you to recognize these elements because they are often hidden, and only the real insider is able to sort them out.

Real Estate Is a Universal Commodity, and All Universal Commodities Are Complicated

I am sure that this is a statement invented by a stock broker. Real estate is found every where, to be sure, but if you think that you can invest in Fort Lauderdale by being the expert in real estate in San Francisco, then you are headed for a disappointment. Trends do follow certain similarities, but they can occur for different reasons and last for different periods of time. What is going on in Fort Lauderdale may not be the same thing that is happening only 25 miles away in Miami. Local trends are really local. Certain neighborhoods suddenly become hot and start to go through a phase of rebuilding. If you get in early enough, that might be the only ticket you need to your fortune. If a local growth phase is nearing an end (because there is no more viable property to buy on which to rebuild), then you need to look at nearby or adjoining neighborhoods that will take off due to the supply and demand effect of the market.

Real estate is so local, in fact, that many people who have had good success investing in their neighborhood have run into difficulty because they believed they could relate that success to anywhere they went. They go on a vacation and fall into what I call the "greener grass syndrome." You know about the green grass on the other side of the fence, don't you? Well, this happens to real estate investors too. What suddenly looks like greener grass than they have at home seems to be a bargain because it is one third or less the price of a similar piece of grass at home. Uh oh, not so! It might turn out that there are too many restrictions, only one fourth the traffic, building and zoning won't allow more than two floors of building, and on and on.

Rely on your comfort zone which is discussed later. The idea is to build your comfort zone in your own backyard first. Expand it and then, if you are so inclined, begin another comfort zone in another neighborhood where, at first at least, the grass looks pretty green.

Chapter 3
What Makes Real Estate Value Go Up or Down

The goals of this chapter are:

To demonstrate the key factors that cause real estate values to go up or down.

To learn how to take advantage of these factors and avoid their downside consequences.

The factors that affect the value of real estate are generally obvious once they are at work, causing real estate to rise or fall in value. It's important to understand exactly what those factors are and how they can cause the value to move either up or down. The key to success in real estate is to use this knowledge in determining when and what to buy, and how to maximize your profit on a sale. Interestingly, the same factor can cause one property to go up in value while causing another similar property in the same town to go down in value, even if it is just across the street.

Ironically, most of the factors do not just suddenly appear. They are elements that have been in place for years, such as local zoning or building codes. Those and other factors may not be noticed or their real impact not unleashed until the owner of a property attempts to take advantage of what he previously thought was the property's real value.

By understanding the six factors covered in this chapter, you will learn to recognize how to take advantage of a situation when it arises, as well as how and when to avoid potential problems that could diminish the value of a property you are about to purchase.

Key Words and Concepts to Build Your Insider Knowledge

Community Planning.

Departments of Transportation

Fire and Health Codes

Lack of Concurrency

Land Use Changes

Condemnation and Eminent Domain

Proceedings Building Moratoriums

Economic Obsolescence

The Rule of Small

Community Planning

Nearly every community in the United States, Canada, and most of Europe has some form of community planning. Within cities this may come in the form of a planning and zoning department that deals with matters such as

"How is this city to be developed?" The county is further controlled by broader mandates from the state, which requires that each county adhere to standards of building and development to fit the scheme of things that the state legislature has decided. Naturally, there is also a higher order of things, and the federal government gets its fingers into the pie through its federal matching funds that local communities vie for funds for road development, bridges, tollways, airports, schools, and countless other federal projects.

Each of these elements of community planning will impose something that may affect the value of your property so that you win or lose value because of it. Because this chapter and others in this book show different ways these factors can affect the value of your property or investments, it is important that you get a good grasp on everything presented here.

The whole concept of community planning is in constant flux, nothing remains fixed. One planning team may be prodevelopment and encourage construction and new urban development, while two elections away a new city council votes to change all zoning laws to effectively stop development in its tracts. Both situations can occur for good reasons, or at least good intentions, but they can have disastrous effects on your property's value, and your rights as a property owner.

Departments of Transportation

Each level of community planning may have a Department of Transportation. This is a powerful factor in controlling development, because development doesn't flourish unless there is good traffic flow in the community. So what goes on in your city will be greatly affected by the planning that is going on in all the different departments of transportation, as well as other departments in city, county, and state planning bureaus. The good news is that, of all the departments in local, state, and federal governments, transportation is the one that can sow your fortunes right under your nose. Once you understand how transportation planning functions, you will be able to avoid most of its potential bite and reap most of its benefits. Why? How?

First of all, understand that decisions and plans of departments of transportation are slow to evolve. Their future plans take years to draft, and years longer to implement. New roads and bridges, and revamping, expanding, and even resurfacing old roads are very expensive undertakings, and when something is expensive it takes a lot of yesses along the way to get final approval. Public hearings are generally required, and the public that shows up not to complain but to observe is the public that will ultimately benefit the most.

World history demonstrates how this works. When one tribe left a foot path marked in the sand, other surrounding tribes began to use it, and it became a traffic way. Soon someone built a trading post at the juncture of two such paths. The Romans were successful because they were greahat it would do to a community if their road went through it instead of through another town 50 miles away. The Romans took advantage of this knowledge and were able to rule vast parts of the world by virtue of the commerce they would bring to an area and the tax they would collect on it. Today, the simple announcement of a new turnpike entrance/exit in an otherwise remote area of the county will bring nearly instant value to the property located at that entrance/exit or it might bring a sudden devaluation of what was once a highpriced, exclusive residential subdivision.

Keep in mind that transportation is not just about cars; it includes pedestrians, trains, planes, and ships. All of these people and goods moving elements of your community are strongly controlled. There are port authorities, airport authorities, the Army Corps of Engineers, and many other departments and committees of both government and quasi government that are quick to stick their noses into any newly proposed event that even remotely concerns them.

Fire and Health Codes

The strongest of all the building codes are usually the fire and health codes of a community. Other building codes may be changed without the requirement of the change becoming retroactive to a building constructed under older codes. But fire and health codes are generally absolute, and it is rare for any building to be grandfathered in (allowed to remain as it is) if one of these codes gets changed. Meeting the new fire or health code can be very expensive. While it might be costly enough in a new building, tearing existing walls apart to install fire sprinklers is both a nightmare and a hunk of change out of your pocket. You will learn to pay careful attention to both fire and health codes.

Lack of Concurrency

This phrase can cause a property owner to shiver on a warm day. Concurrency is a term that was invented by a land planner. Having concurrency means that your property meets all the current requirements to enable you to develop the property more or less as the zoning might allow. If that sentence sounds vague, it is carefully meant to. Most zoning ordinances governing the use of a specific site or tract of land contain provisions that give the local governing body considerable control over the ultimate end product. However, one thing is absolute: If you do not meet concurrency, or if you lack concurrency, then your property may not be developable until you take steps to bring the property into concurrency.

The problem with this concept is it has grown into a many armed monster that can eat developers alive. The simple fact is that to bring a property into concurrency may mean doing something to remedy the traffic congestion that is presently occurring two blocks away from the tract of land like, for example, widen two or three miles of roadway from a two lane to a four lane traffic way. Ouch! An expensive remedy, but not as costly as many I have seen. Clearly, this is an important factor on which you can profit. How so? Well, if you have been following the events of a major new development and discover that the developer is going to have to build a new bridge over a canal to open up a new traffic route to reduce the flow elsewhere, then that new traffic way might be where you want to put your new trading post.

Land Use Changes

Land use is a part of the master plan of the community. This overall plan will designate where development can occur and in what form and density it can be approved. A change to this plan will suddenly change the overall outlook of the neighborhood and the anticipated growth of the market for certain businesses of that community. Any change in any kind of use in your neighborhood, and particularly where you own property, can either jeopardize the value of your property or make you a millionaire.

The sequence of land use plans and modifications to them usually starts at the state level. The state legislators pass an overall master plan for the state, and certain mandates are then passed down to the counties, which have some flexibility as to how they must then implement the plan. The cities within each county then are told, again with some flexibility, how they are to adopt the overall plan to their area. The use of the properties within the city or unincorporated area (county controlled and not within a city) must fit to the overall land use which has been set by this chain of decision making.

If the ultimate land use plan allows flexibility, as often is the case, then it may not be necessary to actually request a change of the plan. However, if the intended or desired use is not allowed at all, then the owner or buyer must look elsewhere, or try to get a modification in the plan. An example of this would be where a property is classified as a retail commercial use. Along comes a buyer who wants to build apartments. If the land use plan allows apartments in the commercial area, then that is okay; however, if it does not (which is more often the case), then the buyer may have to go all the way to the state

One of the key requirements in speculation in land is to pay very close attention to the land use plan and the options available for the use of the land you are thinking of buying. The greater the flexibility of the plan, the more options you might have. Keep in mind, however, that flexibility is not always a good thing. If the ultimate highest price a buyer would pay for a tract of land that you purchased 10 years ago turns out to be for a high end retail use, and the surrounding land to your tract has become low end industrial buildings (great flexibility), then you will lose out. The only way to overcome that potential is either to already know what and who your neighbors are, or to have a large enough tract to be able to buffer yourself from future development that is not up to your standards.

Condemnation and Eminent Domain Proceedings

There are two methods by which a governing body can acquire your property without your permission. The first is by condemnation, and the second is through eminent domain. Condemnation is generally the way a city or community redevelopment authority (CRA) will clear out a blighted area to make way for new development. However, there are certain legal requirements that must be followed, and some states require that the party that is initiating the condemnation or eminent domain proceeding pay for the cost incurred by the owner if the proceeding is contested. Eminent domain proceedings are the usual way that departments of transportation obtain rights of way for new or expanded traffic ways. Each proceeding has the same end result: You sell your property to the agency who wants it, and although you don't have to accept the price, you may end up having to take it unless a court rules in your favor at a higher price.

Building Moratoriums

When there is a rash of development going on, things might be progressing at such a fast pace that the level of services available to the people who live in the area is being outstripped. This happens most often when new roadways have opened up vast areas of vacant land for new housing development. Developers rush in and, before you know it, there are thousands of new residents living in the area, with thousands more likely to follow. Traffic can no longer be handled on the new road, and more are needed now.

Schools don't even exist yet, and forget about things like shopping, fire department and police services, water and sewer service, and so on.

When this kind of situation starts to get out of hand, there are two things the local government can do. It can make the determination that none of the undeveloped property meets concurrency, so it cannot be developed until something is done to remedy that situation; or it can impose a building moratorium. The building moratorium halts the issuance of a building permit in the area chosen until the city planners have been able to sort things out and, at the same time, to slow down the pressure on existing services. Building moratoriums and concurrency issues are difficult to predict, so it is essential that investors of developmental property take them into consideration in their acquisition proposals. The way you do this is to include provisions in your offers to purchase such properties that can protect you as much as possible against the potential delay or reduction of development you will ultimately be allowed on the tract of land. You will do this as a buyer and if you are a seller you will anticipate that a buyer will want to protect himself against such an imposition.

As a buyer interested in building apartments, you have to anticipate that just because the land is zoned for 50 units per acre does not mean you will be allowed that many, if any at all. You might cover yourself by putting a timetable in your offer for approval by the local authorities for your site plan, or even for the issuance of a building permit. If the seller will agree, you can also tie the price of the property to the number of units you will be allowed. This would be your best protection as to the maximum price you can pay, as the price per unit would remain the same if the city allowed you only half what the zoning allows. Of course, the seller would want to protect the minimum price by having a floor (the lowest price he would take) in the deal.

Economic Obsolensce

Eventually every roadway motel gets bypassed by a super highway and just is not economically viable anymore. It may continue to function, but the income stream drops and the value may go down for that reason. An office building becomes old and antiquated and tenants move out to newer and better functioning buildings. A fast food restaurant that was viable 20 years ago is now too small and the operational costs too high for the volume of business it can sustain. These are all examples of economic obsolescence and can present opportunities to you as an investor if legislators to effect a change. This is costly and can take a long time and ultimately it may not be approved anyway,you can ascertain a new use for these properties.

The Rule of Small

Income producing properties are valued by the amount of income they produce. This sounds logical, of course, but its interesting how the Rule of Small affects this concept. The Rule of Small is that small movements in the smallest increment of the income stream will have big impacts on the largest element of the income stream.

Here is an example of how this works: The smallest part of the income stream of a 10 unit apartment complex will be the monthly rent on each apartment. The largest element of the income stream of this same property will be the amount that someone will pay for this property based on the yield required by that buyer. Let's tie that to actual numbers. The monthly rent is $650 per apartment. That rent times 10 apartments generates a gross monthly collection of $6,500 and an annual gross revenue of $78,000. Assume that the expenses for last year totaled $20,000. This would give you a net operating income (income less expenses except for debt service) of $58,000. Ignore leverage for a moment. If a buyer needed to make 9 percent cash flow on his invested capital to purchase the property, he would pay up to $644,444. (I arrived at this by simply dividing $58,000 by the 9 percent: $58,000 ÷ .09 = $644,444).

Here's a recap of this 10 apartment example:

Monthly rent per apartment $ 650

Gross rent per month from 10 apartments $ 6,500

Annual revenue $ 78,000

Income less operating expenses $ 58,000 (not including debt service)

An investor will buy at a 9 percent return $644,444 (maximum price the investor would pay)

Let's assume the investor (perhaps you in another deal) understands the Rule of Small as it applies to real estate. It is clear that to increase the bottom line return of this property, there are only certain things that can be done without changing its use:

■ Increase rents. The best way to increase the bottom line is to provide for annual increases in rent. Some leases are tied to a cost of living index, or some other outside benchmark index. In these instances, any increase in that index will cause the rent to go up by the same percentage. If no such provision exists in the lease, you will have to wait until the tenant wants to renew or otherwise renegotiate the lease.

■ Decrease expenses. Good management can accomplish a lot to attain this goal. The key is not just a reduction of expenses, but a reduction of the overall ratio of expense to the collected rent.

■ Leverage the transaction. By obtaining financing that costs you less than the desired return on your investment, you will obtain positive leverage. The money you borrow will decrease the amount of capital you have invested, so your ultimate return is leveraged up.

■ Do a combination of the above. A mix of more than one of these elements will generally be the target any new owner should seek to accomplish.

Let's look at these four strategies in action. In our 10-unit apartment example, say the investors can do a little of each of the value enhancing techniques. The rents are bumped up to $675 a month, the expenses are cut by $300 a month, and 80 percent of the price can be OPM from a local savings and loan at an 8 percent total payment of principal and interest per year. Here is the new economics of the deal:

Gross rent $ 81,000

Less the new expenses $ 16,400 ($20,000 less $3,600 of reduction)

New net operating income (NOI) $ 64,600

Annual cost of debt $ 41,244 (principal and interest of the new

$515,555 mortgage)

New cash flow $ 23,356

Capital invested $128,889

The investors are going to borrow 80 percent of the purchase price needed before the changes, which was $644,444, so the loan will be

$515,555. The cost of this debt is 8 percent of that amount per year, or $41,244. This leaves the investors with a cash flow at the end of the year of $23,356 (NOI of $64,600 less $41,244 of debt service equals $23,356 in cash flow). Here is the recap thus far into the deal:

Price $644,444

Loan $515,555

Cash invested $128,889

Cash flow $ 23,356

Return on cash 18 percent (18 percent of the of $128,889 cash invested)

The investors purchased at $644,444 and borrowed $515,555 so they have only invested $128,889 of their own capital. On this they earn $23,356 in cash flow each year. That is a return equal to a touch over 18 percent. So the Rule of Small has done it again. The investors went from an anticipated return of 9 percent to 18 percent with some very modest changes in the economic structure of the deal.

Every rental deal you get into will have the same potential. Sometimes the move to a better leveraged investment does not occur overnight. However, it may occur the very next day after you close. How so? Well, what if you negotiated the above purchase, but the deal was that you would close in six months. In the meantime you would take some of the cash you were going to put down at the closing and use it to make some improvements to the property.

Improvements that can quickly show returns are interior and exterior paint (especially the front door), new landscaping, a nice new stone walkway, and similar sorts of things. You do this prior to closing in fact, you do this prior to getting your mortgage commitment. Now the property looks different. You might even have rented out a vacant space or two at a higher monthly rent than the other tenants are paying, which shows the lender that higher rents are likely. Now, armed with a new proforma at higher rents, you borrow even more money than did the investor in the above example. Every deal will have the potential to allow you to increase rents and decrease the ratio of your expenses to your gross revenue. Remember, you don't even have to actually reduce expenses, only the proportion of expenses to the total revenue. Small wins every time. You will see a lot more of this in action throughout this book.

Six Primary Factors That Make Real Estate Value Go Up or Down

There are six primary factors that can cause the value of any real estate to rise or fall:

1. Supply and demand

2. Local zoning

3. Changes in infrastructure

4. Economic obsolescence

5. Maintenance procedures

6. Motivation to buy or sell

Each is discussed in detail here as to how and why it changes the value of real estate. You will quickly discover that the same property may be impacted in either direction by the same factor. A change in infrastructure, like the widening of the road in front of a strip store, can cause a sudden downturn in value as tenants move out or go out of business, but a year or two later that new roadway can causethe value to jump to a higher level than it originally was. The timing and duration of the factor can play an important role in how you time your acquisition or sale of the subject property. Let's look at each of these factors from the following angles:

- General comments
- Effect on value (increase or decrease)
- How to take advantage of the situation
- Pitfalls to watch out for

Supply and Demand

General Comments: The supply and demand effect tends to balance itself out in the long run. However, there is always a period at each end of the cycle when there is either a greater demand than supply or a greater supply than demand. It is important, when viewing a potential supply and demand situation, that you make sure you are looking at all apples, or all oranges, and not a mix of the two. For example, in a hot market there can be several things going on at the same time. All expensive homes in the million dollar and up range can be in great demand with a moderate to low supply, while townhomes below that price might be overbuilt and the demand for such properties waning. This would suggest that an ideal time to buy a townhome is just around the corner and that it is likely a great time to sell a million dollar house.

Effect on Value: Whenever there is a strong demand for a product, its value will go up. It is a good idea to examine the situation, however, to ascertain what has created the current demand that did not exist previously. If expensive high rise condos are the hot ticket right now, what caused that? Have drug smugglers found this a great place to do business? Are people retiring to the area in greater numbers because the air above the ground floor is more healthful than at firstfloor level? Or is it that no new high rises have been built for a long time, and that newness of product has always been in demand but there were none available to buy?

Newton found out that what goes up also comes down, but when it comes to real estate, that fact may not have any real bearing on your future profit or loss. You have already seen that you can profit nicely even when you sell for less than you paid for a property, but it helps to make even more than you paid. Property values are relative, however, and the true test of value is what you can buy once you sell. Too many people overlook that factor and put a big profit in their pocket, only to find that there is nothing in the marketplace that they can purchase to replace what they just sold. Therefore I always caution investors when they get excited about a profit or despondent over a potential loss of value.

The supply and demand cycle is just that a cycle. If the investment property is still throwing off a return you can live with, then hold on to a declining value if there is a good reason for the downturn, and if the light at the end of the tunnel a change in the cycle is just around the corner.

How to Take Advantage of the Situation: As I just mentioned, it might be a good idea to ride the down cycle through its course if you find that you are well into it. If, however, you are just entering the cycle, you may want to consider making a move before the situation worsens, if you can. If you are in a really hot market, it is usually easy to see when the end is coming. All you have to do is to check out how much inventory is either available or being planned. If the product is flex space (warehouse/office buildings), a quick review of industrial vacant or redevelopment land available can give you a good clue as to how long the rise in redevelopment will last. If there is a shortage of available land, the new development will come to a sudden halt and prices in the existing product will go even higher. This will occur because the demand will continue, until the high prices cause developers to open up other areas that are not too distant from the present area. Then local prices may stabilize or even drop as cheaper product comes available elsewhere. This concept can be applied to any kind of real estate use.

In almost any situation, there are opportunities to be had. A strong demand will eventually cause one of two events to happen. The first is that developers will run out of new sites to develop and the unspent demand will open up other areas. If you know that the current hot area will run out of development sites, then be the first (or one of the first, anyway) to find a new area that will offer opportunity for new product at a better buy. Keep in mind this new product will need to overcome the distance from the hot area by offering a similar or better product at a lower price.

The other possibility is that the demand will continue, and more and more supply will be developed in anticipation of the demand, until there is an overabundance of supply. Bam! the hot market suddenly slows and things even out. You will have anticipated this and already be looking for an infill location and a new kind of product that will cater to the people who are occupying all these flex space warehouse/offices. (In fill locations are areas in the heart of existing communities or development where old buildings are torn down to make way for new product.)

Pitfalls to Watch Out For: The interplay of supply and demand is a factor that rarely exists by itself. There are almost always two or more factors occurring at the same time. One of the most critical outside influences to fuel the supply and demand cycle is the suddenloss or considerable reduction of the supply side of the equation. I say "sudden" because it may appear that way to the general public while not actually being sudden at all. For example, the city rezones a major area of land, currently zoned for industrial use that allows flex-space development and changes it into low density office park zoning. This will not spur new office park development unless that was already a hot issue, but it sure will affect the flex space market that is soon to be hot by decreasing the supply of that product. Be wary of well intending government officials.

Local Zoning

General Comments: As I stress use over any other single determinant of the ultimate value of real estate, zoning becomes the critical factor that all investors must take into consideration. Zoning is an ever changing element that goes through evolution within a city. When the city fathers are development prone and embrace every new project with open arms, the codes and their interpretation may be relaxed; whereas when one or two of the city commissioners are voted out and new ones replace them, the mood changes and antidevelopment is the rule of the day. Because zoning is so important, be sure to pay close attention to the "pitfalls" section of this category.

Effect on Value: Zoning and the building codes that regulate what actually is buildable are far more critical to commercial real estate than to single family homes. Why? Because the codes are tougher and more comprehensive. A home owner can, in most areas of the country, install a well system for drinking water without being required to test the water quality. But if the property is a hotel or restaurant or any business operation, the well water would have to be tested, and if it were found unsuitable for consumption, another water source (bottled water or a water purification system designed for commercial use, for example) would need to be provided.

Zoning is in constant flux that is, it is going through evolution and change. This means that what you were able to do with your property 15 years ago when you purchased it may not be the same today when you want to tear down your old motel and put up a brand new Hampton Inn. For this and many other reasons (specific to each unique combination of area, current zoning, and intended use), consider zoning to be a potential pitfall you must overcome. New interpretations of the code are made by zoning board members as well as city commissioners, none of whom may be experts in the field, and who may have no experience in investing, developing, or financing a project like the one they are nonetheless about to either turn down or approve.

Yet zoning is also a grand opportunity that awaits the investor who takes the time to study how it can be used. Those potentials for profit will come to anyone who can learn how to look beyond the fact that a neighborhood is made up of small frame homes that were built 70 years ago and realize that the underlying zoning allows multifamily homes with a mix of commercial areas in between. These are the places where dreams are formed, goals realized, and fortunes are made.

How to Take Advantage of the Situation: When you truly understand the zoning ordinances and building codes of your comfort zone, you will discover that it is the guidebook showing you where to look for your commercial investments. The example of old single family homes sitting on land that is zoned for high density, multifamily properties is real. Many cities have these areas right in the more valuable parts of town the center of town. Individual lots and building sites can be assembled, allowing a developer or investor to end up with entire blocks of high density real estate. The creation of a large building site where only small lots existed before is not the result of rocket science. Mind you, the zoning was there all the time. The homes sat there for

40 years or more, but no one really paid attention to the situation until you did.

Let this be a good example of why the steps to wealth are almost never seen by most people. The more you know about what is going on in your backyard, the greater the opportunity you will have to recognize where to dig for your gold.

Pitfalls to Watch Out For: There are many factors, however, that create difficulty when analyzing zoning. First of all, the terminology or classification of zoning differs greatly between communities. Cities within the same county may have similar zoning classifications but the interpretations of what they allow can differ greatly. An R-4 classification might mean four units per acre in one city, whereas RMM4 might be the counterpart zoning in the adjoining city. Some zoning classifications, such as a B-3 zoning, might be the most flexible commercial and business zoning in one city, but in an adjoining city it might be one of the least flexible. The key is to know the applicable zoning codes and what is allowed and not allowed.

Yet even when you think you've figured out what you can do, you may notice a small asterisk by the words "minimum setback" and 10 pages later discover that setback is tied to height, and that the higher you go, the greater the setback. These are what I call "gottcha" terms, and they can be hidden within the code not entirely because the planners want to hide them, but because they get added years after the original code was drafted. When it comes to zoning (and anything else that is governed by the city or county commissioners or one or more of their departments), you must keep abreast of not only the codes and ordinances, but how they are applied to situations that parallel your own circumstance.

Be sure that any purchase agreement you present to a seller gives you the right to withdraw from the agreement if you are not able to use the property as you want to. Be sure that your intentions have been well documented in the purchase agreement so that there are not legal complications later if you need to withdraw from the deal, if you are turned down by the appropriate department. As a seller, make sure that a buyer does not lock you up for a period of time longer than you are willing to wait if problems arise in this or any issue where future approvals (building permits, occupational licenses, special exception approvals, and the like) are required.

Changes in Infrastructure

General Comments: A change in any infrastructure can have a rippling effect on the value of real estate. I have already used several examples of this kind of value changing factor, such as new or expanded roadways, or bridges that bring traffic, good or bad, to an area. A new stadium, a playhouse, a new park, all these things will have an impact on the value of some real estate. Some will go up in value while others will decline.

Effect on Value: Because this factor is long in planning, the real estate insider will have ample time to consider how the change will affect the surrounding area, or to decide whether another, more distant area will benefit more from the change. The beauty of this factor is that the results from infrastructure changes are very predictable. What happens to the surrounding property when a mega shopping center is built? Where do the values go in any neighborhood that suddenly gets a university or a big expansion of the downtown government center? New roads, bridges, airports, schools and whatever else that has happened in the last few months, or has been announced as planned in the near future, will have an effect on property values. The key is to know which values will go up, which will go down, and why. To ascertain that, all you have to do is check out what happened elsewhere in similar circumstances. History will repeat itself of that you can be sure.

How to Take Advantage of the Situation: You will be able to take advantage of a situation only if you have become aware of it. This is a dilemma with most of these factors. They can slip past you and by the time you know what is going on, it is too late to get the maximum benefit from the situation. You learn about changes of infrastructure at the same governmental offices where you find out about zoning and the city fathers' approach to future development. Remember, nothing happens with respect to changes in any infrastructure within a city that has not followed a process of public meetings. Anyone can keep informed by attaining these meetings. The most important of these meetings are city and county planning and zoning (P&Z) board meetings, city and county commission meetings, and new development workshop meetings (where the developer and the P&Z staff often try to satisfy the public and work out differences at the same time). There are other meetings that are noteworthy, but start with just your own city meetings first and go from there.

When you discover, at a P&Z board meeting, that a developer is planning a new amusement park on the north side of town where old man McDonald's farm is located, you might just want to take a ride out that way and start checking out property values. Remember that it is essential for you to be more than just observant at these meetings. Take the opportunity to meet the people, not just the commissioners and the board members, but the other important people in the room, and, most important, all those fellow real estate insiders who are already members of that exclusive club you are in the process of joining.

Pitfalls to Watch Out For: Government changes too. Appointed members of boards resign and the faces of everyone you ever saw sitting on the dais at one of these meetings will eventually be replaced. Not only are they gone, but there may be new comers who have ideas and approaches different from those the former members had. This means you have to play it close, meet the new members, and learn which way they lean and how they are apt to vote when it is your turn to seek their approval for a project.

Economic Obsolescence

General Comments: I have touched on this factor earlier in words and concepts you need to know. It is one of the major factors that causes slums and brings about urban renewal. What is built and not maintained will deteriorate, just like the Roman Empire, and just like the housing project that is let go to ruin. But it is also more subtle. It can be an entire community that does not keep up with the times. Traffic flow goes to pot, the inner city starts to get run down, and people begin to move to the suburbs, leaving the downtown area even worse off than before as the spiral of devaluation increases. I've seen many cities where this has happened. Likely, so have you.

Effect on Value: Flip a coin, call it opportunity or chaos. Economic obsolescence is one of those natural events that allows for a renewal of thought and of use. The impact of this factor depends on how widespread the obsolescence is. If it is only one or two buildings then the problem is best seen as an opportunity. The value of the property affected by economic obsolescence will go down. This allows a buyer the chance to purchase it with room to improve the existing structure, or to buy it for the land value and start all over again. Economic conversion, refers to the opportunity to transform an existing property when its current use has less economic viability than a new use for the same property. This is a good way to go with many properties.

How to Take Advantage of the Situation: I just gave you one answer. Economic conversion may be the best solution, but it is not the only one. In economic conversion you turn to our good friend, the zoning that is applied to the property, and review all the possible uses that can be put on that property. If none look promising, then visit with the head of planning and zoning and ask if the city staff would support an alternative zoning for that site. Remember, responsible government will not want to see economic obsolescence take hold, and the quicker they can introduce a more viable use, the better it is for everyone. They might actually agree with this statement and help you get a zoning that lets you be the one to make that introduction. As I have mentioned earlier, zoning is ever changing.

Some of these changes are made by the city at staff recommendations. Other changes are made at the request of a property owner. Economic conversion may work best with a change in zoning to allow more flexibility in the future use.

Some examples of economic conversion include an old Victorian home that you can turn into several nice medical or legal offices; an old, single story motel that becomes an antique mart; and a closed "big box" (any big building like an old supermarket, or department store also called a "big black box") that becomes a multiscreen movie house, a mushroom farm, and so on.

Pitfalls to Watch Out For: I touched on the first pitfall earlier, that is anything to do with zoning and building codes must be approached very carefully. Some other pitfalls appear with closely related problems such as parking codes and fire codes. Both of these can be expensive to deal with if they become major issues in the remodeling. The word remodeling introduces something else, namely that the cost to remodel anything can get out of hand very fast. If you don't have detailed as built plans, or if the building has been remodeled in the past and no reliable plans for that remodeling are available, every time you remove a wall you can be in for a big and very expensive surprise.

Maintenance Procedures

General Comments: Let it run down and pretty soon the whole neighborhood runs down with you. The approach you take to maintenance should fit with your goals of investing in the property.

Effect on Value: It's a downhill trip for the property that is not being well maintained, unless there is a good reason for the lack of maintenance. If the management posture is to just keep it producing for a little longer until you tear it down, then that strategy might be okay. For example, when you buy a property with the idea to remove the existing buildings in ten years or so, it might be easy to let the property deteriorate while getting every dime of rent you can. However, this may initiate a downward turn for the neighborhood, which will adversely affect your future development. Poor maintenance under any circumstance is not a good idea. I would recommend that you protect the surrounding values by at least keeping a good face on the property. If you don't, you may not be able to stop that downward spiral for the surrounding properties.

How to Take Advantage of the Situation: Whenever I see a property that is slipping down the maintenance hill, I make a point of checking with the owner to see if they want to sell and at what price. You will be surprised at the reasons people let well located properties go into such a state: no money, out of town or state owners, so deep in debt and so out of shape that even the bank doesn't want the property, and so on. Often the property is owned by someone who just doesn't have the time or patience to deal with it. Interestingly, this same owner may not even want to deal with the process of selling the property. Root them out and you might get the buy of the year.

Pitfalls to Watch Out For: Today toxic mold is one of the worst nightmares you will ever face. A rundown property, especially one with roof leaks, may have that problem. It can be dealt with, but the remedy is expensive, so the new use for this property has to be a good one.

Motivation to Buy or Sell

General Comments: You have heard about the wolves being able to smell trouble, which is why they are suddenly at your door when you are down on your luck. That is part of the factor of motivation. When you are forced to sell is the very time that no one wants to come close to the price you need. It often doesn't matter how realistic your asking price is. On the other hand, when you are the most qualified buyer, the seller might try to hold you up for a price greater than what anyone else would pay.

Effect on Value: The answer to this is not so obvious as you might think. A seller who is highly motivated to sell may hide the reason for this motivation from the very person who is trying to help him his broker. I have had many clients who were clearly so motivated to sell that you could smell it a mile away. Why were they so motivated? I heard dozens of the wrong reasons. Why the wrong ones? Many people are embrassed to acknowledge they have failed at something. Also, they didn't want other people to know just how desperate things had become, either with a marriage, a health issue, job problems, debt up to their ears, or the bodies buried in the backyard. I have heard them all, but rarely the real reason.

Values go down when you show urgency, unless the market is so hot and your property so ripe that nothing will stop a buyer from paying a decent price. Buyers who are logical about the situation often do all they can to hide the fact that they actually want to buy.

There are lots of ways to protect yourself in this situation. As a seller, try using an out of town lawyer or broker, as an example. But if word of your motivation gets out, then you might have to step up and accept the penalty in the form of a lower price.

How to Take Advantage of the Situation: Let's look at the two situations. Say you are a desperate, highly motivated seller, whatever the reason. What should you do? My advice is to take a step back from the property and the problem and look at the reality of the situation. Do you really need to sell at all? You see, most people believe that selling the property is their only way out. Divorcing, so gotta sell; moving to the other side of the world for a new job, gotta sell; wife is having triplets, so gotta sell. The dog dug up one of the bodies, gotta sell (okay, with this one, by all means, sell). All the reasons that exist should be reexamined. Perhaps the property should be rented out, or perhaps a joint venture with a local investor to do an economic conversion would prove interesting, or a real estate exchange for another property in the town where you are moving to. All of these are options that many people fail to look at.

The worst part of this situation is that many people let the real reason for this desperation fester to the point that someone else makes the decision for them. That is called foreclosure and it hurts. So look at all the options and talk out the real problem with your broker. If finances are part of the dilemma, then talk with the bank or the lender and see what can be done. Believe me, banks do not want to foreclose, but they will if a solution is not offered them.

For the potential buyer who might be faced with paying too much, there are some fine tactics that can help with that situation. One is called, "I'll pay your price if you accept my terms." This gives the seller the opportunity to brag about holding you up at the closing for big bucks, while at the same time you smile because you got terms that made it work for you. Sometimes the situation requires some hard negotiations to take the phantoms out of the picture. Who are the phantoms? They are all the other people the seller is telling you are out there trying to buy the property. If you know you are being asked to buy at a price that you think is too high, then put your lower offer on the table and give the seller a "take it or leave it" proposition.

You can always say, "I was only kidding."

Pitfalls to Watch Out For: The biggest pitfall for both sides of the motivation factor is to let emotion get in the way of a sound business deal, and to let it go to the point that you are not the one in control of the deal. I have sweated out many deals, both mine and my clients, where the motivation was so strong that all the other side of the deal had to do was get a hint at just how strong it was and the deal would go south. Buyers would not meet the asking price or anywhere near it, or sellers would hold out for price and terms that were not realistic. I don't have much sympathy for buyers or sellers who let that happen to themselves, so never let a deal die because you got too emotionally involved.

Chapter 4
How to Build an Effective Commercial Real Estate Comfort Zone

The goals of this chapter are:

To provide you with the steps necessary to establish your comfort zone to illustrate how and where to locate your comfort zone.

Your comfort zone is similar to a child's favorite blanket or stuffed animal. For a young child it provides comfort in the middle of a hectic day, as he cries himself to sleep. For you it is the relaxing realization that you are in your own territory, where no one can intimidate you, and where no one knows the terrain better than you do. In real estate investing, your comfort zone is that place you have chosen to be your farm of investment properties. It is where you will seek and find your fortune.

This chapter is dedicated to getting you started on the right foot. It is designed to give you all the steps you should take to pick the area, tips on what will make that area really work for you, and then a map of how to proceed to make that zone the single place you know like the back of your hand.

Concepts to Build Your Insider Knowledge

Listing Services

FSBO

Active Listings

Tax Assessor

Map Quest

Zoning map

Listing Service

Your local board of realtors and other real estate groups have sources of their listed properties that you can freely access anytime you want. Check with any realtor about this, and look for those free magazines that advertise real estate for sale in your area. They are often found on curbside racks near full service restaurants and other businesses frequented by tourists. This information source will provide you with data that can be helpful to you when you start to review the local real estate market. Local news papers often have a weekly section devoted to recent sales, with the names of both buyer and seller and the price of the property sold. Start clipping these out when you see property that is in your designated comfort zone.

FSBO

This is pronounced "fizz boe" and means "for sale by owner." This is an invitation to meet the owner of a property that you might want to buy. Even if the property is not something you would like to own, if it is in your comfort zone, call the phone number on the sign or announcement anyway, and start meeting the people who own property your comfort zone. The more inside information you get, the better it will be for you in the long run.

Active Listings

These are listings the local realtors are actively working. They are not sold, pending sale, expired, closed, or canceled (the other potential realtor listing classifications). Of the total list, the ones that are the most interesting are listed as active, closed, or expired. The active listings are those properties that are currently on the market. The closed listings are interesting because there will be information tied to them that tells you what, who, and how much the property actually sold for.

The expired listings can be a hidden gem. These are listings that didn't sell but eventually the original listing expired. They may have been relisted at a lower price, or they may now be free game for anyone who wants to track down the owner. Expired listings always raise the interesting question: Why didn't the property sell? If the seller was motivated before, he might be nearly desperate by now. Check these listings out when you come across them. If you are working with a realtor, then alert your realtor that you want to concentrate on the expired listings. Believe me, realtors will thank you for taking this tactic, because those listings do not belong to another real estate office so they won't have to split the fee with another sales team.

Tax Assessor

The tax assessor and his or her often very large staff maintains the property records of most communities. This is a county level position, so once you meet the tax assessor and get to know how their office works, and what a gold mine of information they are, you won't need to meet another until you go to another county. Slowly tax assessors' data is becoming available on the Internet and the information is getting easier to obtain. In most of the Florida areas where I prospect my investments and listings, I am able to sit at my computer and in seconds find out the names of the owners of a property, when they bought it, how much they paid, who the seller was, who the original owner was that took the vacant land and built the building, and a wealth of other information.

Keep in mind that every transaction that takes place where documents must be recorded, like property transfers, for example, is public information and will be available to you free, and usually without difficulty. In areas where the data is not yet available on the Internet, you may have to pay a visit to the tax assessor's office, but that is not a painful event. You will want to learn the ins and outs of this source of information as quickly as you can. There are people in these offices who will walk you through the computer programs (if they have them) or their card or microfilm files. When you are being shown the ropes of the system, be sure to make good notes of what you are learning so you don't become a pest who can never seem to remember what you did last time.

MapQuest
MapQuest is just one of many different mapping programs on the Internet. You reach

their home page by going to www.mapquest.com. Once you are there, you might have to play around with it until you get the hang of it, but it is relatively simple. MapQuest will give you a detailed map of just about any place in the United States. You can zoom in to get a close up, or expand out until you can see the entire state or states around the location you chose. There is also a section you can instantly switch to that will show you an aerial (if available) of the area. This simple and free source of data would have cost thousands of dollars a year to access a few years ago, but now it is free. Use these sources and make note of the ones that are most friendly and give you the best information for your area. While this information is generally accurate, any data network of this size can have glitches or improperly programmed information. If the data is critical, it is a good idea to double check important information with more than one source. Search the Web for other "Map" web pages; there are several others that may provide better results for your specific need.

Zoning Maps
Each city and county has zoning maps of the real estate that is solely within its jurisdiction.

The maps are usually not free but are never really costly. They are detailed enough that you should be able to find any property within the prescribed area without much difficulty, although sometimes you will need the help of a magnifying glass. These maps also include a section where the different zoning codes are scattered about on the map, with a brief description of what each code represents. Remember that these descriptions are basic and will never tell you the whole story.

For example, under a general heading of "Residential Zoning" you might find a list that starts with R-1, then R-1a, R-2, R-4, and so on. Next to each of these will be a brief description, like "R-1, single family low density;" "R-1a, single family cluster;" "R 2, duplex" (two units), and so on. Believe me, you don't know much yet, and to learn more you will have to get the building and zoning code book for that specific city or, if it's an unincorporated area (not within a city limit), for the county. Unfortunately for the computer illiterate, these codes have been brought up to hightech levels and might be available only on the Internet.

The bad news even for the computer literate is that these codes are usually cumbersome to deal with because of the amount of information you have to absorb. Worse, however, is the fact that the full scope of rules that govern any single property is almost never found in one section. An example of this is where a zoning code indicates that in a B-2 zoning you can also build anything allowed in B-1 zoning. Okay, so you look at B-1 zoning, and it tells you that B-1 will allow anything which is also allowed in C-3 zoning, and so on.

The best way to deal with city ordinances and building codes is to have a printed version of the building and zoning codes buy it, or get a computer friend of yours to print out the one on the Internet. Only with this book, and frequent updates that contain changes to the printed or Internet versions, will you be able to get the whole of the printed story. In other words, all you can get is what is printed. How it is interpreted by those who regulate and control these ordinances and codes may be another story in itself. I won't get into that right now, but as you read this book you will see examples where what the code says is not entirely what the city fathers will allow. That is one of the major issues with building and zoning codes that frustrates many investors as well as professional land planners.

I advise you to make several copies of the zoning maps of your area (maybe more than one page), as you will eventually need more than one copy. Copies of large zoning maps can be obtained at a blueprint facility, which is where architects and engineers obtain copies of large plans and drawings. This will generally be less expensive than purchasing several copies from the original source.

Elements Common to All Initial Comfort Zones

The specific elements of your comfort zone will have to be defined by you. These elements will be the categories of property you most want to include in your investment portfolio, the general price range of those properties, and their level of rental potential (already at the top, needing some improvement, or real fixer uppers). I will, however, illustrate what makes up a good zone and how you can establish the boundaries of that zone to maximize its benefits to you.

Some elements are universal to all comfort zones. I will list these as they apply to your first comfort zone, as the first such zone is the most important. Later you can relax some of the criteria about to be listed, but for now, stick to the following four:

1. Close proximity

2. Limited number of opportunities

3. Within one governing area

4. Well defined area

Close Proximity

Choose an area close to where you live and work. This proximity will let you drive through the area every time you travel to and from work. Vary your routes as much as you can, and you will begin to see things about the area you have overlooked before. These things will be opportunities that will soon begin to stick out like sore thumbs.

Limited Number of Opportunities

Design each comfort zone so that it does not contain so many properties that it overwhelms your ability to learn about them. As your knowledge in zoning and other codes grows, you will be able to expand the area.

Initially the zone should contain a minimum of several hundred of the category of investment properties you believe you would like to own. Keep in mind that you don't have to narrow your investments down to one single kind of property. Be a bit flexible, particularly in the beginning. Later on, as you find you are more comfortable with one niche of property over another, you can begin to specialize. I know people who consider themselves to be "Mr. Gas Station" or "The Fast Food Brothers" or "Rental Apartment King." Other investors branch out into different kinds of real estate. Let your natural feel for the property tell you what best suits your talents and abilities.

Within One Governing Area

Your first comfort zone should be totally within one governing area. By keeping the properties within the same city or county unincorporated area, your research and study will be confined to one set of rules and regulations. You want to limit the number of meetings you go to and zoning ordinances and building codes you need to learn.

Once you master this zone then expand it, staying, if possible, in the same city until you run out of properties to buy and need to branch out into another area.

When you do expand, try to first expand the existing zone by simply adding area that is adjoining. If that is not possible or beneficial, due to the lack of the category of property you are interested in, then try to stay within the same governing area.

Well Defined Area

Mark your comfort zone on the city zoning maps so you always know when you are there. It will be tempting to constantly expand the zone, but you must resist expanding it too quickly. Let that happen slowly until you come to a natural boundary. This might be a main street or the end of a specific subdivision. Keep the areas small at first, and work them until you know everything possible about the history of the area, the current market values of the properties it contains, and the potential for the area or parts of to improve in the future.

Key Factors to Becoming an Expert in Your Own Backyard

The following five key factors will aid you in becoming an expert in your comfort zone:

1. Learn the simple things.

2. Get the right tools.

3. Keep records of important data.

4. Research what happened in success stories.

5. Build walls around your comfort zone.

Learn the Simple Things

Remember, your goal is to get to know everything about the zone you will chose. This is 90 percent becoming aware of what is going on, meeting the people in the zone, getting to know what factors can affect the value of the real estate in that zone, and 10 percent relating what you learn to a specific area of your zone.

As you begin to absorb everything you can about the value of the property in the zone you will, slowly at first, begin to see opportunities where previously you only saw a run down building. The actual learning process will occur as you make the commitment to start attending the planning and zoning board meetings. This is where new development projects are first introduced to the public. After one or two P&Z meetings you will want to begin to attend the City Commission meetings, as this is where those projects might get discussed and voted in or out.

The people you meet at those meetings are the present members of the unofficial real estate insiders club. Get to know them, just as you will get to know the mayor, the staff members of the city planning and zoning departments, the building department officials, and the other members of the city commission. All the members of the planning and zoning board volunteers appointed by the commissioners are the first line of attack (or defense, depending on your point of view of any project) and can have an important effect on what goes on.

The people who make presentations at these meetings or speak for or against any of these projects will be the developers, their lawyers and experts, and those who are against the projects, along with their lawyers and experts. All these people will become your teachers as to the elements that govern your comfort zone.

Get the Right Tools

Prior to attending any meetings, it is a good idea to obtain the initial tools you will need. You can obtain most of the items or information from the area building

department, the city hall, or other departments within the city. The tools to start are few. Here is the initial list:

■ The city zoning map and the book of the building and zoning ordinances and codes which you will get from the city building and zoning department.

■ A list of principal characters, with full names and phone numbers, which include all the city commissioners, and the city manager, and city attorney; head of the building department; head of the planning and zoning department; head and members of the planning and zoning board; county commissioners.

You will be able to get this list from the appropriate departments. If you run into any snag, my best suggestion is to call the office of the mayor, ask for his or her secretary, and introduce yourself as a real estate investor new to the area. Explain the list of characters you need to obtain addresses and phone numbers for, and ask the secretary or assistant who might be the best person to help you. You will get help. Once you have these tools and information, you are ready to start meeting the principal players. As you begin to narrow down your comfort zone, you will find the zoning map and codes essential to the ultimate selection of the area.

Keep Records of Important Data

Your record system can be as elaborate or as simple as will work for you. The key in the early stages is to meet people and let them get to know you as a real estate investor. They will later assume (rightly so, by then) that you are, in fact, a local real estate insider. However, you will need to make note of important people you meet or see in action at the city and county meetings. As you drive around your potential comfort zone, make note of what you encounter. What is for sale, whom to contact, and so on will all become important later on.

As you discover phone numbers and names of owners or brokers, make contact with those people. Do not worry if the property in question is not what you want to invest in.

This is your fact finding stage, and you need to learn about all the property in your zone. You should become an avid reader of the business and real estate sections of the local newspaper. These will be filled with information that at first won't appear to be important to you. Then one day you meet one of the people interviewed, and it turns out they own a property in your area. Start programming your onboard computer (your brain) to track the events of your community.

A good source of information for years to come will be your photographic record of the events in the zone. If you don't currently own a simple 35 mm camera, or a digital camera, then buy one or the other. Whatever it is, it should be easy to operate and small enough to fit in your coat pocket. As you see properties that are for sale or have recently sold, take a photo of them. On the back of the photo be sure to note the date, the property address, the legal description, the property owner at that date, the asking price, and the sold price. All this information will be easily obtained and will create a historic record of what has been going on in your zone. In just a few years you will have visual proof of what kind of trend is occurring in your area.

Always take photographs of property you own at regular intervals, say at least once a year. You will be surprised how fast time flies and how differently a well maintained property matures compared to those that are just barely kept in operation.

Research What Happened in Success Stories

You will often hear or read about how someone developed a new shopping center on the other side of town, or filed for a permit to build a high rise office building in the center of town. These are success stories you should pay close attention to.

How did they come about? Who were the players? Be curious about these events because you will probably cross paths with these people at some time in your investing future.

Build Walls around Your Comfort Zone

You want to keep the area small enough that you can effectively become an expert in that area. Nothing that goes on in the zone should be excluded. In the box is a list of factors that you should get to know. Although some of these factors may appear to have little to do with your investing in any category of real estate in the area, I can assure you that each and every one will play some role, no matter how minor. While this list is rather comprehensive, it may not include certain elements that are particular to your community or your comfort zone. You must remember that the success of any commercial real estate venture is dependent on the acceptance of the project by the local area, the attitudes of the people who work in the venture, and the patrons of the businesses, or those who rent the apartments or facilities.

Review this list and type or write it out as a checklist of the things you need to be aware of to insure that you are learning everything possible within the walls of your comfort zone. Consider each item on this checklist as it would apply to any property in your zone. Remember that different zoning codes may have different applications of these items. Be

sure to learn each variation, or at least know where to quickly find the answers. Most of the answers will be found in the zoning or building code books, or by calling the appropriate city department.

Learn How to Let Your Computer Lead the Way to Your Success

If you are not computer literate right now, then after you read this paragraph, stop and make your next goal to learn how to surf the Web for information. You don't have to own a computer, but even a used one will be worth the investment, and it does not have to be loaded with bells and whistles either. There are computers available for public use at libraries and satellite libraries around town, so get with it. You will be very glad you did.

There are many ways to start to build an address book for Internet information sources. The best way is to start with the most effective source you will use, the tax assessor's web page. This source is full of data you will need in order to be on the top of your real estate investment game.

Your Comfort Zone Checklist

Building setback minimum allowed by zoning code

Building heights allowed by zoning code

Commissioners (city and county) for the zone

Emergency plans for storms or other emergencies Fire codes

Fire stations serving the zone

Libraries serving the area

Master plan for transportation and traffic ways for the zone

Nearest emergency room and hospital

Public transportation

Public parks in the zone

Residential density per acre allowed by zoning code

School districts

School locations

Shopping areas for the zone

Storm or emergency shelters

Utility upgrade plans for the zone

Zoning codes

Almost every developer who has a reputation to protect has a web page. Usually, in the local real estate section of the newspaper, somewhere down at the bottom of their advertisements, they will print their web or e-mail address.

You can start to search for other sources by going to the "search" line of your Internet browser. Ask for almost anything and you will generally get many potential sources. Spend a moment looking for what appear to be the best sources, those that are govern mental or institutional and not just advertisements. Check out only the important looking ones, and save the advertisements for a day when you have absolutely nothing better to do.

When you find a source that proves to be valuable to you, mark it as a favorite (that little red heart in AOL, or just "favorite" in most other Internet browsers) so you can get back to that site easily. If you can, form a file, say, "Real Estate Data", and save those web sites as favorites in that file on your computer.

How to Choose Your Comfort Zone
The actual process of choosing your comfort zone is depicted in the following nine stages. These nine steps should be treated as an overall process that takes place simultaneously, rather than as a series of individual steps that must each be accomplished prior to moving on to the next

one. The following list outlines the stages, each of which is then discussed in detail.

1. Pick two categories of real estate you want to own.

2. Discover what kind of zoning allows that use.

3. Review the city zoning maps for that zoning code.

4. Highlight the areas of town with that zoning.

5. Drive around town and decide what areas appeal to you.

6. Combine one or more areas until you have a minimum of 100 properties.

7. Mark the boundaries of these areas.

8. Watch for notices of public meetings or homeowner meetings pertaining to your zones.

9. Begin to become an expert in each area.

Pick Two Categories of Real Estate You Want to Own

It doesn't matter if these are the two categories you ultimately end up with. The key here is to get started with something. My suggestion is that one of the two categories should be tied to a need you have right now. Are you renting? If so, then why not include small apartment buildings as one of those categories? Many real estate investors have started out owning and living in their own rental apartment building. I know from experience that it was a great way for me to start. If you are in business for yourself or with others and rent your place of business, then a strip store or industrial complex might fit the bill to satisfy that need. Whenever you can stop paying rent and apply that capital to your real estate, you are ahead of the game.

Discover What Kind of Zoning Allows That Use

Once you have chosen two categories of real estate, dig into the building and zoning code books and find out which zoning categories will allow that use. You are likely to find more than one zoning category that will work, as it is usual for some uses to be progressive in a specific zoning. In other words, you can build a house in single family zoning but also in multifamily zoning. Going up the line, you can build a low density apartment building in medium density zoning, and a medium density apartment build ing in high density zoning. So cover all bases. By the way, when you are driving around and you see a small, single family home, do not assume that the zoning is limited to small, single family homes. Check it out; it might also allow a high rise office building.

Once you know the different zoning categories or codes that you will need for the real estate you want to own, carefully go over the zoning map and make note of where these zoning categories can be found. It is likely that you will recognize some of the parts of town where you see these zoning codes, so you might rule out some of the areas you don't want to start with right away. But I caution you about doing this too early. If we are talking about investments and not personal residences, then do not be too particular early in the game. Great investments are often those that cater to the middle range tenant, as there tend to be more of them than the super rich tenants.

On the other hand, if you want to start out with the high end of whatever the real estate is, that is fine—however, it will narrow your selections.

Highlight the Areas of Town with That Zoning

Using a yellow highlighter, mark on the map the areas you want to scout out. Then drive around to review the neighborhoods. This is your chance to see what

is going on in parts of town you may have never been to. Remember, this is a scouting expedition and needs to be given time and effort. A fast drive around town will not do. You should make note of any property that is for sale, for rent, or marked "sold." Check out the ownership and sales history of those properties. The ones that are for rent are especially important because they will give you an insight as to the income potential for the area.

As you begin to travel into other parts of town, you will find that the rental market and prices of properties that have sold have gone through some changes almost every time you visit the area. Ask yourself why. What is it about one area that makes the obtainable rents different from other areas of town? Don't try to rack your brain for the answer; ask the owner or a realtor who has a property for sale in that area or another area. Use their already loaded brain cells and save time.

Drive around Town and Decide What Areas Appeal to You

After you have made some preliminary scouting expeditions into different parts of town that fit the required zoning for your chosen real estate venture, then begin to narrow down the area or areas to create your first comfort zone. Be sure to mark each area clearly on your zoning maps. Remember to make several copies of the blank maps, as you will need many along the way.

Combine One or More Areas Until You Have a Maximum of 200 Properties

These will be separate properties made up of the two or more categories of real estate you have selected, plus properties that may not fit the category but are located on properly zoned lots. For example, if your choices are small professional buildings and midrange apartment buildings, you might luck out and discover that in some areas the same zoning works for both uses. As you drive around, with the zoning map on the seat next to you (or in the hands of your trusty spouse, who can become a very important assistant in this process), you can start to make note of the older, need to be torn down properties that would be good locations for exactly what you want to own.

Mark the Boundaries of These Areas

Once you have made the selection of the initial comfort zone, mark the boundaries on the zoning map, and make several copies of the section you are going to turn into your investment gold mine. Enlarge the sections to a scale where you can make notations on the map. Your notations could be as simple as small numbers that refer back to a master sheet of information.

Watch for Notices of Public Meetings or Homeowner Meetings Pertaining to Your Zones

One way to do this is to be sure you get copies of the agendas of appropriate public meetings sent to you. Again, turn to the secretary of the mayor and ask him or her how you would do that. If you have an e-mail address (get one if you don't), they might be able to e-mail you the dates and agendas for every meeting. With the agenda in your hand, you can pick and choose which meetings to attend and which ones to skip. There will be meetings where absolutely nothing will seem to be of interest. However, I have never failed to benefit somehow from attending a public meeting.

The local homeowners' associations (HOAs) might be a little more difficult to locate, but they are listed somewhere, and the mayor's secretary will know where. Those associations are made up of homeowners or property owners in the area or people who have an interest in the area. They discuss what is going on and frequently have the developers of a pending project come and make presentations to them. This is so important, in fact, that most planning and zoning boards and commission meetings insist that the developers conduct such meetings to make sure that the local property owners are aware of what is happening. The voice of the neighborhood has been able to stop many projects cold in their tracks.

Begin to Become an Expert in Each Area

The process will move much faster than you think. Let me explain why. Take a look at the neighborhood where you presently live or work, or both. What do you know about what is going on there? Do you know the names of your neighbors?

How about what they paid when they bought their properties? Or what they pay in real estate tax? Or the direct phone line to the nearest emergency room? Or where your employees would catch the bus to get to where they live? Odds are you struck out on most if not all of these questions. But you would not be alone.

The beauty of this process is that you will know more than the property owners and those who live there. This is a big boost to your confidence in learning about any specific real estate market area. And never underestimate the effect that eyeballing an area during your scouting expeditions has in building your knowledge of these areas. Real estate is a must see, must feel commodity. You can not get the true picture from a photograph, it is impossible. It takes a physical visit to a property to get to know it. Its value is based not just on what it looks like, but how the whole neighborhood shapes up, what kind of traffic flows through the area, who works there, and who comes there on business. Spend time in your comfort zone and it will treat you very well indeed.

Chapter 5
How to Accomplish Effective Due Diligence

The goals of this chapter are:

To Illustrate What You Must Know Before You Buy, Build or Lease

To Show You the Easy Steps to Ascertain This Data and What to Look For To Give You Directions to Turn to When Things Turn Up Less Than Sweet

Due diligence is a term that few people used 20 years ago. Back then it was simple: You were allowed to make inspections, and if everything looked okay, you'd go ahead with your plans. But times change, and prices are getting higher and legal problems more costly to deal with, no matter if you are the buyer or the seller. The word of the day is caveat emptor (let the buyer beware). This applies no matter what kind of real estate you are buying, and especially with commercial real estate, because consumer protection laws that give home buyers some legal rights against sellers who violate those laws generally do not apply to investment property of any nature. You must be cautious and assume that the worst can happen even when dealing with noncommercial property.

In one recent Florida court case, the judge ruled that a residential condominium was a commercial property because the buyer planned to rent out the apartment. Because it was now a commercial transaction the buyer could not claim protection under laws of willful misrepresentation by the seller, even though the seller had lied about certain violations. The decision was based on the fact that as a commercial transaction, the buyer had been given ample time to make any and all inspections possible, and he had signed a contract that indicated the property was to be purchased "as is."

In this chapter I show you what you need to know before you buy, build, or lease; what you should do to go about getting the information; what problems you might find and where they can hide from you; and what to do once you are faced with those problems. It is essential for you to understand that commercial real estate presents far more problems when it comes to due diligence than does residential real estate. First of all, the laws of most states are very strict as to disclosure of known problems with residential real estate but much less strict in the area of commercial or investment real estate. Also, because you are apt to be dealing with leases and other contracts that are going to be a part of the investment package you are buying, these elements increase the amount of time required and the number of experts you may need to add to your due diligence team.

I want to caution you about the legal responsibilities that you think the buyer or seller or their brokers might have in any real estate transaction. Laws that deal with fraud, misrepresentation, outright lying, theft, and that sort of thing will vary from state to state. But no matter what wrong is done to you, the ultimate problem may not be who is in the right but how much it will cost you to try to get a remedy. Legal actions of almost any kind can be long, expensive, and stomach acid–forming, to say the least.

The best thing you can do is to keep your eyes wide open and learn to do your due diligence with a fine tooth comb. If you can walk away from buying a property that even hints at having problems, then either make sure the problems are cleaned up, paid for, or dealt with to your satisfaction, or walk from the deal. Life is too short to walk into a deal where you know something smells wrong and you try to tough it out. So what about deals that people close on every day without ever having done one tenth of the due diligence this chapter stresses as essential? Well, fortunately, most people are honest, and most deals don't have problems, but why take that chance? Do your due diligence, with gusto.

But another word of caution: Avoid making the mistake of doing extensive and expensive due diligence without having a signed agreement that ties up the property. The reason should be obvious, but if you don't see it, take note: There are many sellers who don't want to give prospective buyers sufficient time to make these important investigations. Unless you feel you know so much about the property that you don't need to do such inspections, then pass on properties where sellers balk at reasonable due diligence periods in purchase contracts.

Key Words and Concepts to Build Your Insider Knowledge
Due Diligence by Definition

Letter of Intent

Formal Agreement

Inspection and Review Period

Environmental Inspections

Easements

Encroachments Code

Violations

Zoning Use

Allowed Use

Due Diligence by Definition
Due diligence is the process you perform prior to having your purchase contract go "hard." It goes "hard" when you reach a point where you have something other than

your time and inspection fees at risk—perhaps a deposit, or a promise to close on the property without further inspections. Until then, in essence, you are asking the seller to take his property off the market with nothing more than a contract and perhaps a deposit that would be refundable if you decided to walk from the deal.

The amount and extent of the inspections and reviews you do to satisfy yourself of the condition of the property, buildings, and title will depend on what you are buying and what you intend to do with the real estate after you buy it. If it is a vacant tract of land that you don't have a clue what you will do with other than sit on it and hope it goes up in value, then your amount of due diligence will not be very extensive nor time consuming. On the other hand, if the property is an old shopping center you plan to tear down in the hope of getting apartment zoning to build affordable housing, you will have a lot of issues to investigate. The word extensive can be misleading. In fact, everything you inspect or review will be extensive. There is no such thing as inspecting for lead and only looking in half of the rooms of the building. The same is true for asbestos or other hazardous elements.

Do not be afraid of due diligence. All of the detail work can be done by firms that specialize in the different areas of due diligence that I cover in this chapter. I provide a detailed list of things that need to be inspected and reviewed, but a lot of the items on this list will not apply to your intended investment at all, whereas, some items on the list will apply to all properties that have buildings or other improvements on the land. The snake that can bite you is not the inspections and reviews that are done by the inspection teams you hire, but what they tell you they don't inspect. Pay very close attention to this aspect of due diligence. Know what you need, and know what you are getting. If those two lists don't match, then get the missing elements taken care of before you move forward.

Letter of Intent

This is the form that begins most negotiations on commercial properties (on many homes, too). It is exactly what the term indicates: a letter that shows the intentions of the buyer. The sample letter given here covers the important bases.

A Simple Letter of Intent

Dear Property Owner,

My name is John Brown and I am a real estate investor from Fort Lauderdale, Florida. In a recent visit to your area I became aware that you may consider selling a shopping center you own. I would like to purchase that center and I will pay you $10,000,000 cash at closing. The closing will occur 60 days following my approval of my due diligence, and I will have a reasonable time to complete the necessary inspections. This time will be detailed in the formal agreement once the seller has supplied the buyer with property data.

If I do not approve of my due diligence inspections and review for any reason whatsoever, then I may withdraw from the contract, and any deposits placed in escrow by me, as indicated by the terms of the contract, will promptly be refunded to me. If this is acceptable to you (the seller), then so indicate below and I will have my lawyer draft the formal agreement for your review. That document will be in your hands within five working days from your notice to me that these or any other mutually acceptable terms are accepted by both parties.

As this is a letter of intent and not a formal contract, no binding agreement to purchase and sell will be in effect until the parties have executed a formal agreement. However, both parties agree that they will act in good faith in the negotiations of this agreement, and if this or a subsequent letter of intent is acceptable to both parties, the seller agrees not to negotiate with any other party for the sale of this property for a period of 30 days so that the formal agreement can be drafted, reviewed, and, if acceptable, executed.

If I don't hear from you on this matter by noon this coming Friday, then this letter of intent shall be considered null and void.

Sincerely,

John Brown

Letters of intent can be as simple as this, or much more detailed. The point is to nail down the most important business decisions right up front. If you don't like my price or terms, say so or make changes to see if I will go along with them, or forget it. The letter of intent should not attempt to illustrate more than price and terms and one or two other important issues. The details of an agreement will be outlined in a more formal state after this business end of the deal has been agreed to. At that time the agreement will be expanded to include the legal issues of the sale and the specifics of arriving at a closing.

Formal Agreement

This is the legally binding document. It is the purchase agreement, the final contract between the parties to accomplish what the letter of intent started. I use the term legally binding but that is only partially true. The buyer generally has certain provisions and a timetable to conduct the due diligence portion of the contract. Those elements will contain out provisions or escape clauses that will allow the buyer to withdraw from the agreement in the event that some problems with certain aspects of the property turn up during the inspections and reviews. Even if no problems turn up, those provisions usually allow the buyer to walk for any reason, provided that notice of that decision to do so comes within the time provisions of the due diligence period.

Sometimes the seller has an opportunity to terminate the agreement if the buyer fails to timely accomplish certain elements of the due diligence, or the seller doesn't like the results of a credit report on the buyer (usually this is requested if the seller is holding a mortgage or note from the buyer). Remember, whatever the contract says, provided the terms are legal, establishes the obligations and penalties to which each party must adhere. A word of caution: Do not expect the other side of any negotiation (buyer or seller) to "do the right thing" or have sound business ethics. You may hope for this, but there are people who have no scruples and until you get their signature on the contract, you do not have a deal (unfortunately, not even then in some situations).

Inspection and Review Period

This is the due diligence period or timetable. Its length depends on the nature of the property and the ease with which inspections can be scheduled. A complex due diligence may take a much longer time if the property is remote (say in the islands somewhere, or in a small town where everything has to come from a larger city a great distance away). Environmental inspection provisions, discussed in the next section, are often drafted to allow for extensions of the due diligence timetable in the event an initial inspection uncovers a potential problem that can only be researched properly with additional inspections.

Environmental Inspections

Environmental inspections are exactly what the term suggests: inspections to ascertain if there are any environmental issues that need to be addressed. Some of these potential problems are deal killers, as it can get very expensive to remedy an environmentalproblem. This would be the case with discovery of a hazardous issue.

There are many facets to environmental inspections. Some deal with protected areas, wetlands, areas that are off limits due to the presence of certain plant and/or animal life, dangerous conditions that either exist currently, or might come to exist if you tear down a building (such as one that is full of asbestos that will become airborne), and so on. Rather than attempt to list all these problems and perhaps miss the most important one for your area of the world, let me suggest that you contact any of your local environmental inspection companies and discuss the situation with them. This tip goes for any inspection you might choose or need to make.

Easements

Easements are rights that others have to access, pass, or use property, and in other ways possibly make it difficult or impossible for you to use land you thought was yours. They should show up on a good recent survey, but they don't always get picked up by even the best of surveyors. Some of these easements are classified simply as utility easements which are designed as passages through or across a property for the placement of any of the usual utilities, such as water, electric, gas, telephone, cable services, and so on. There can be other public easements prescribed by law or city ordinance that can get skipped in a cursory investigation either by a lawyer or a surveyor, so it is a good idea to check with the city building department and public works to make sure there is not something unforeseen that could blow your project out of the water.

Encroachments

An encroachment is where something protrudes from another property into your property. Usually the encroachment is a building that a survey should clearly show. However, you can have a hidden encroachment that is underground. This happened to me once when a property adjoining one I own was occupied by a local fire department. When I purchased the property, the surveyor made a mistake and placed the south border line 20 feet north of where it should have been. The problem got worse because, prior to my buying the property, the fire department had built a building and installed a septic tank that had a drain field on what they thought was their property but which was actually mine. They had relied on information given to them by the same surveyor. When I wanted to build on this tract of land I discovered the error in the survey, and later my contractor discovered the septic tank. The fire department was expecting the county to take the south 20 feet of my property to resolve the problem, but the county didn't like the prospect of getting into a lawsuit over such an issue.

In any event, it still took me nearly a year and several thousand dollars of legal expenses dealing with the city, county, and, of course, the fire department. All worked out in the end, and it was all over something that would never have been found by anyone had we not discovered the survey error.

Code Violations

When some aspect of a building does not meet the current building and fire codes, as well as any other city ordinance or zoning code, you may be in violation of that code. I say violation because it is possible that you may not meet the code but may still be allowed to maintain the building as it is because you met the code at the time the building was constructed. This works for zoning and some (but not all) building codes. This situation is called a nonconforming use.

Code violations are usually a matter of record, but the difficulty is, whose record? Not all cities function the same, and fire code violations might be dealt with in one department (I would try the fire department first) whereas a building code would likely show up in the building and zoning departments. Any code violation can be a problem but the worst are usually the fire codes, because there is no grandfathering in on those codes in most parts of the country.

When you hire a general building inspection company, they may or may not also check for code violations. Be sure to ask, because if they don't, you may have to farm that task out to someone else. I recently had a good lesson in how this can lead to lots of problems after the closing. I brokered a sale to a long time client of mine and it turned into a mini nightmare. It was a well located office building, and the seller indicated he had partners and wanted to sell because he could not work with his partner friends any longer. (This happens sometimes when you have great social friends and you bring them into a business deal and the friendship goes down the toilet.)

Not long after we closed on the office building, I suggested that we put the building right back on the market. A quick profit was the motive, if I could produce one. Along came doctor whats his name and bought the building, paying my client a clear $100,000 profit after all costs and fees. All was fine for about a year, and then suddenly there were threats of fraud, accusing my client of not disclosing certain elements of the building to the doctor. A foreclosure suit was filed by my client, who holding a second mortgage on the building, which the good doctor had not paid. Then, countersuits were filed, and so on.

It turned out there were some outstanding code violations from the fire department. These violations had been filed on the former owner, and when they turned up, the cost to remedy was, according to the doctor, so high that, had he known about them, he would never have purchased the building.

I won't get into all the details, as the case has yet to be settled. All I can say is that in Florida and many other states, when it comes to commercial and investment real estate, the buyer had better beware. In essence, if you have the time to make your inspections, do so—especially if the contract has an "as is" provision, which warns you, "Hey, you are buying this just as you see it. Make your inspections, then take it or leave it." This is not as harsh as it sounds. Almost all investment real estate is sold on this basis, just as most used cars are. However, unlike with most used cars, you as buyer can have considerable time to make inspections and review everything prior to purchase.

The good doctor had these opportunities and hired two inspection teams to give him a report on the property. He could have hired a dozen, as he had ample time to do so. The contract said "as is," and on top of that, the seller gave him a credit of around $18,000 to handle any problems that might occur with the building. This was the seller's insurance that if there were problems they should be covered.

Well, those code violations surfaced the next time the fire department inspected the building and, like a bear to honey, they were after the good doctor to make the necessary repairs.

The point is, no matter where your legal rights are, no matter how much you try to satisfy either the buyer or the seller, depending on your position in the deal, legalities can be the end result. My suggestion, following this experience, is this: If you are a seller, give a letter to the buyer, listing all the items that you think the buyer should inspect. If you have any hint of a problem, make sure you have that category listed. Always list code violations that you are aware of.

Zoning Use

Every zoning classification has a list of possible uses that would normally be permitted within that zoning. It is important to read the zoning codes very carefully, because many of them allow uses permitted in lesser zonings. For example, in a high density multifamily zoning category, which is one of the most unrestrictive multifamily zoning categories, you may also be allowed to build a mid rise low density building. On the other hand, if a property is zoned low density multifamily, you could not build a high rise without going through a change in the zoning or obtaining some other permission. While some commercial zoning also allows multifamily use, multifamily zoning may not allow commercial uses but may allow professional offices. The more you know about the exact zoning and what it will allow, the better your chances of spotting a windfall in the form of an allowed use that will give you added income, and therefore increased value.

Allowed Use

The use the city will allow for a specific property may differ from the use the zoning says is allowed. Why? Because it can exercise one of the "gottcha" clauses in the zoning or building codes. The key is to find out what potential gottcha clauses might exist and then explore them until you are satisfied with your findings. In all developmental property, I recommend that a buyer condition his actual purchase on the approval of a site plan (and, in some large projects, the building plans), which includes the use approval by the planning and zoning boards and the city commission. If the use they approve is more limited than you thought you would get, then you have several choices: Take what they gave you, fight for what you want, renegotiate the contract, or walk from the deal. I say more about this later in this chapter.

The Eight Most Important Elements of Due Diligence

1. Assume nothing told to you by the seller is correct.

2. Hire qualified building and land inspectors.

3. Audit all leases.

4. Obtain inventory list and double check it.

5. Review all contracts.

6. Get a recent certified property survey.

7. Make sure title is valid and all liens and debt are verified.

8. Properly set the due diligence timetable.

Assume Nothing Told to You by the Seller Is Correct

If this sounds cynical, it is. I'm not talking about factors of trust and honesty. Many sellers do not know what problems exist, so they will say that none do. That is not sufficient information on which to base the decision to proceed with a multithousand or multimillion dollar investment. The safest thing you can do is to ask if the seller has any documentation, such as prior inspection reports or recent surveys, that would show the status of the property.

Hire Qualified Building and Land Inspectors

Getting good inspections might be difficult. Some inspection companies are great for homes but not so great for shopping centers and absolutely horrible for large apartment complexes. Look at their references. Check with past clients. Go back several years, because that will be where unknown problems surface. If you get marginal responses from past clientele, forget that company and move on to another inspection team.

Audit All Leases

This is something that you may not be qualified to do or want to spend the time doing. You should hire a property manager or accountant versed in commercial

leases of the same category of real estate as that being inspected. If all the leases follow a standard format, you may want to have a real estate lawyer review one of the leases to make sure there are not some potential problems with the terminology that was used. It is possible that a former owner came from another state and used a lease that was okay in his home state, but for your state the lease violates tenant rights. Do not attempt to audit a lease unless you have special knowledge in lease terms and conditions.

Have the leases audited and then verified as current. Verification is done through an estoppel letter, which the seller must obtain from all the tenants and which is attached to a copy of the current lease. This letter simply states that the attached lease is a true and accurate copy of the existing lease and that no other agreements have been made between the tenant and the owner. The letter will also spell out the status of the lease and when the last payment was made. If you discover later that the estoppel letter was not correct, you will have a claim against either the tenant, the former owner, or both.

Obtain Inventory List and Double check It

This is the real drudgery of many large commercial closings. I especially hate having to go through a 400 room hotel, room by room, to verify that each item is actually in the room and is in good condition. But you or someone you hire should be responsible to do this. I recommend that in addition to a visual inspection of this kind of inventory, someone makes videotape of it as well. That is one of the best bits of evidence to fall back on, if done properly.

What is the proper way to do a videotaped inventory? I start the tape by verifying the date and location of the inventory inspection and introducing the parties who will accompany the inspection. At least one of these persons will be from the seller's team. As I approach a location, I announce it so that the tape picks up the verbal introduction to the room. If it is a hotel room, I videotape the entry of the room with the room number clearly showing. Several of the inspection chaperones will be inside the room and will show up on the film as the room is slowly scanned so that every item is seen while also being called out. If any of the items that should be there are missing, they are mentioned. If anything is not working or is in need of repair, that is shown and stated.

So far, none of the inventories that I have conducted in this way have led to any dispute over what was missing later on. Be cautious with any kind of investment that has a major inventory, as it is easy for thousands of dollars to slip through the cracks of the deal with sloppy inventory taking.

Review All Contracts

Contracts will include leased goods or fixtures, repair contracts, employment contracts, service contracts, insurance agreements and contracts, legal representation, obligations on municipal bonds pledged to cover local tax assessments, and so on. If the property is part of a condominium (a condo office building, for example) there will be obligations that come with the property, such as assessments imposed by the homeowners' or property owners' association, or other maintenance agreements. If you, as buyer, have the risk of becoming responsible for any of these agreements or contracts, you need to know what they are. If you disagree with them, you must do so within the due diligence period and seek a remedy from the seller. This is not something you can do after the closing and still expect to get full satisfaction.

Get a Recent Certified Property Survey

A proper survey should show the legal address of the property, its lot, block, and sub division, or metes and bounds description, in addition to the street address. All the property dimensions should be clearly noted, together with the exact location of any buildings and their outside dimensions. All utility easements and any other possible easement should be noted. If the property has any recorded deed restrictions, those should also be noted.

Of these items, the one that is rarely shown is a deed restriction. If any exist, they are imposed by a previous owner, often the developer of the property. Sometimes, by local laws, deed restrictions expire after a certain period of time, but in some cases they never expire. Deed restrictions are important because they can contain any whim a previous owner decided to impose on the buyer of that property. This can include things such as greater setbacks than the city ordinances require, no buildings less than a minimum square footage (which may also be greater than what the city requires as a minimum), and a multitude of sometimes silly things. If there is a recorded deed restriction, be sure the surveyor includes notation to it on the survey.

The real danger with a survey is that a problem may be there right in front of you and no one catches it. Why? Because most closing agents (lawyers, title companies, banks, and the like) do not compare the survey to the property. Consider that a surveyor is hired to do a survey of a specific property. The surveyors aren't aware of what you know or don't know about the property, so they go out and correctly and accurately perform their job. The survey is passed on to the title company, which reviews it for things that may affect title—encroachments, easements, violations (such as improper setbacks of buildings on the property), and that sort of thing. The title company may elect to exclude certain elements from their title coverage, in which case you and your lawyer may seek a renegotiation of the deal. But beyond the normal things that a title company can check with their computer, they (and most all closing agents) will assume that all else is okay. Lawyers then look at the survey and, just as with the title company, they may pass it on as proper because the title policy shows no problems.

So far no one has taken the survey out to the property and asked, "Is what I see when I am at the property what is shown on the survey?" Often that is not the case, and yet the problem was there to see all the time, if you knew what to look for. Let me give you two examples of how serious this can be.

I wanted to buy a lot in Fort Lauderdale on which to build a new home. One criterion I wanted to fill was the lot had to be within a couple of blocks of the beach, and it had to have a deepwater boat dock (ocean access without fixed bridges) so I could dock my 40 foot sports fisher behind the house. I liked one lot because of its location, but I had ruled it out when I walked the lot with a measuring tape. Measuring along the seawall, I found that there was only 25 feet of frontage along the canal, which was too short to allow a dock for my boat.

The lot was odd shaped, mostly rectangular, with a piece that extended down to the water of the canal. Two surveyor nails had been driven into the concrete header of the seawall, and each had a faded yellow circle around it. Landscape hedges from the two neighbors came down to the seawall just outside those marks. My assumption that those nail markings showed the actual water frontage was the same as perhaps thousands of other people who had walked down to the canal and then ruled out that lot.

A year went by, and one day I was at the county tax assessor's office and happened to look up that specific lot. I had the clerk pull up the plat of the subdivision and made a copy of the lot, blown up several times its published size. Later that afternoon I took a walk around the lot and paced off the boundaries as the plat showed them to be. Lo and behold, if the plat was right, a large amount of the landscaped area used by the neighbor to the north, plus another 25 feet of seawall, actually belonged to this vacant lot.

I researched the history of the sales of the property to the north and discovered that in the past 7 years the house north of the lot had sold three times. That seemed strange yet logical when everything came together. People had been buying the house to the north problem was there to see all the time, if you knew what to look for. Let me give you two examples of how serious this can be.

I wanted to buy a lot in Fort Lauderdale on which to build a new home. One criterion I wanted to fill was the lot had to be within a couple of blocks of the beach, and it had to have a deepwater boat dock (ocean access without fixed bridges) so I could dock my 40 foot sports fisher behind the house. I liked one lot because of its location, but I had ruled it out when I walked the lot with a measuring tape. Measuring along the seawall, I found that there was only 25 feet of frontage along the canal, which was too short to allow a dock for my boat.

The lot was odd shaped, mostly rectangular, with a piece that extended down to the water of the canal. Two surveyor nails had been driven into the concrete header of the seawall, and each had a faded yellow circle around it. Landscape hedges from the two neighbors came down to the seawall just outside those marks. My assumption that those nail markings showed the actual water frontage was the same as perhaps thousands of other people who had walked down to the canal and then ruled out that lot.

A year went by, and one day I was at the county tax assessor's office and happened to look up that specific lot. I had the clerk pull up the plat of the subdivision and made a copy of the lot, blown up several times its published size. Later that after noon I took a walk around the lot and paced off the boundaries as the plat showed them to be. Lo and behold, if the plat was right, a large amount of the landscaped area used by the neighbor to the north, plus another 25 feet of seawall, actually belonged to this vacant lot.

I researched the history of the sales of the property to the north and discovered that in the past 7 years the house north of the lot had sold three times. That seemed strange yet logical when everything came together. People had been buying the house to the north

problem was there to see all the time, if you knew what to look for. Let me give you two examples of how serious this can be.

I wanted to buy a lot in Fort Lauderdale on which to build a new home. One criterion I wanted to fill was the lot had to be within a couple of blocks of the beach, and it had to have a deepwater boat dock (ocean access without fixed bridges) so I could dock my 40-foot sports fisher behind the house. I liked one lot because of its location, but I had ruled it out when I walked the lot with a measuring tape. Measuring along the seawall, I found that there was only 25 feet of frontage along the canal, which was too short to allow a dock for my boat.

The lot was odd shaped, mostly rectangular, with a piece that extended down to the water of the canal. Two surveyor nails had been driven into the concrete header of the seawall, and each had a faded yellow circle around it. Landscape hedges from the two neighbors came down to the seawall just outside those marks. My assumption that those nail markings showed the actual water frontage was the same as perhaps thousands of other people who had walked down to the canal and then ruled out that lot.

A year went by, and one day I was at the county tax assessor's office and happened to look up that specific lot. I had the clerk pull up the plat of the subdivision and made a copy of the lot, blown up several times its published size.

Later that after noon I took a walk around the lot and paced off the boundaries as the plat showed them to be. Lo and behold, if the plat was right, a large amount of the landscaped area used by the neighbor to the north, plus another 25 feet of seawall, actually belonged to this vacant lot.

I researched the history of the sales of the property to the north and discovered that in the past 7 years the house north of the lot had sold three times. That seemed strange yet logical when everything came together. People had been buying the house to the north thinking it was on a larger lot and had a much greater frontage on the seawall than it actually did. How had the landscaping come about? The original builder of the house, who had landscaped the lot, had also owned the vacant lot at the time. What happened after that was failure on the part of at least those three succeeding owners to properly check the legal description of the lot with the actual "what do I see" version.

I purchased the lot, then sent the neighbor a case of what his wife said was his favorite beverage, prior to having my surveyor drive little wooden stakes down the real property line. Gone was his beautiful hedge, outdoor stone barbeque grill, and 25 feet of his seawall and dock. I was the beneficiary of doing my homework. The other example was what happened to Mr. L, a well known apartment builder in the South Florida area, who purchased a lot on which he planned to build an apartment complex. The seller owned several lots in the area, and Mr. L chose one that suited his dream apartment complex. A survey was made, and everything seemed to check out. The legal description that showed up in the contract and title policy matched the survey, the dimensions were exact, and everyone, including the seller, signed off on the deal.

A couple of years later Mr. L, who was living up north at the time, had a set of plans drawn up and spent several thousand dollars getting the lot ready for construction. Trees had to be cleared and the lot needed fill, so tons of that were ordered and delivered, and the small building in the rear was torn down.

"Wait!" Mr. L must have screamed when he saw the bill for that item. There had been no small building in the rear of the lot. "Oh no!" the seller must have screamed when he drove by his lot and noticed all the action going on, and the demolition of the artist cottage that he used when he was in the mood to paint. Where was Mr. L's lot? A block away. The seller's lawyer had sent the closing agent a legal description and survey on another property the seller owned, and no one ever checked it out.

Make Sure the Title Is Valid and All Liens and Debts Are Verified

Not every document is absolutely correct, no matter how legal it looks and how genuine it appears. You may have heard the saying, "Don't buy the Brooklyn Bridge," which stems from an early con game in which a company was set up to sell shares in the Brooklyn Bridge that links Manhattan to Brooklyn. People who bought such shares ended up owning a worthless document.

There are many things that can affect the value of title to a property and not be part of a con game, so it is critical that you have a title company or your lawyer search the title for anything that might hint at a problem or, worse, show a cloud on the title. A cloud on the title, as it is called, is evidence of an outstanding issue that does not appear to have been closed. Such an issue could be the death of an owner without legal notice of that effect, or a prior sale that indicates there was a mortgage taken back by the previous owner in a foreclosure suit, but there was no satisfaction of that mortgage in the records. Some of these matters are errors, misfiled documents, or documents that were lost somewhere between the delivery to the clerk of circuit court and the actual recording of the document. Sometimes a party shows up as an owner, but no one has gotten that person's signature on the contract you are holding.

Get these things straight. Often the title work is done only at the last minute. However, in commercial transactions many of the inspections and other due diligence work is far more time consuming and expensive than the title search. Because of this, I recommend you have all the title work done early. If problems do show up, the seller will have additional time to get things straight prior to the actual passing of a clear title to you. Title searches are an essential method of checking for any recorded easements across the property too. It's a nasty surprise if you find out at closing that there is a sub way under the building you intended to tear down.

Properly Set the Due Diligence Timetable

Timetables for due diligence are generally referenced in the formal contract as 45 days, 60 days, or some longer period of time. They may also have extensions, as I have mentioned earlier, that provide for more time if certain inspections are required, or if the seller drags his or her feet in making certain disclosures or delivery of certain documents necessary to accomplish the inspection. Then, somewhere else in the contract, in a paragraph that is unrelated to the due diligence issue, is a sentence something like this: "In this agreement all days referenced will be construed as business days, which exclude weekends as well as nationally recognized holidays when the majority of banks would be closed."

That simple sentence now turns calendar days into a much longer period of time. That is okay, if you understand it that way and agree to it as the seller. As a buyer, the longer you have to do your due diligence the better it is. Make sure that the contract is very clear on that point. Often a buyer will put in a sentence that makes the change from calendar days to business days in the hope the seller doesn't catch it, so look for some provision that does exactly that, often in the most unlikely place of the contract.

The Four Elements to Prepare for Due Diligence

1. Ascertain what to inspect and/or review.

2. Select the inspection team(s).

3. Make sure all aspects are covered.

4. Carefully debrief the inspectors.

By now you are pretty well primed on what you need to look for in your due diligence and you are ready to set the process in motion. I have broken this procedure into the following four steps.

Ascertain What to Inspect and/or Review

Make a note of the critical elements of the property that first caused you to select it—size of seawall, how many units you want to build, how many floors, and so on. Those factors should be absolute to you. If those criteria aren't satisfied, then nothing else matters. But how well will your plan for the property fit, and what costly elements will you face? Those issues must be covered in the balance of the inspection. Discuss this matter with two or more inspection teams if this is your first time up at bat in this part of the world or with this category of real estate. Ask what unique things should be inspected. Be sure that code violations, deed restrictions, and other easements are on the list.

Select the Inspection Team(s)

Based on what you need to accomplish, choose the inspection team or teams you will need. They will include the property and building inspectors as well as a title insurance company or lawyer to review the title of the property. Make sure that you understand the limits to which any of these members will inspect. If they leave out something, then find another inspector who can do that part, or do it yourself if you feel able to.

Make Sure All Aspects Are Covered

Remember the data on the survey problems. This is the most overlooked aspect of all. Don't wait until you get past your due diligence period to make this kind of a comparison. It is easy for you to miss out on something if you let all the inspections go on separately without some coordination. Your lawyer is checking the contract, the title, and that sort of thing. But if you are not aware of the problems that he or she has uncovered, there may be another complication that should have been double checked but wasn't. Be sure that all the inspectors have actually seen the property. That is the only time they may notice that something is missing, like where is the lease for the super market on the site.

"Oh," says the seller, "that is on an out parcel," which means it is not included in your deal. And all the time you thought it came with the property. Or it might be something less obvious, such as, did you know there was a land lease under part of the real estate? Worse still can be a long legal description that is difficult to read due to its metes and bounds descriptions. In the end the title turns out fine, but it did not cover all the property you thought you were buying. This could be similar to a missing out parcel, or several buildings that you also thought went along with the center.

What happened? Well, someone forget to give you the lease, and your lawyer or the title company didn't know about it. They assumed that the legal description on the contract covered the total property.

Carefully Debrief the Inspectors

Carefully read the report, then go over it with the inspector or head of the inspection team. Make sure you understand everything stated, and ask about the consequences to any potential problems the report might raise. Later on, be sure to have each member of the team read the summary of the results of other inspectors. Ask them this question: "Based on those other reports, is there anything you would like to reinspect or anything in your report that you need to change or modify, or anything that you think the other inspectors should reinspect or change or modify based on what you have found?" Do this with all of them, including your lawyer, and your accountant (if a review of financials and or leases and contracts were a part of the inspections). Make sure that each member of the inspection team knows the timetable in which you have to give a "go forward" approval to the seller, or stop the deal right then and there.

Eight Things You Can Do When You Find Problems

The following list gives you eight options to consider when you find problems. Perhaps your initial assumption of the problem was an overstatement and it will work itself out relatively easily. Or the initial problem you uncover could turn into a nightmarish quagmire of one problem growing into another.

Review this list of options—it might take you all eight to discover that the last one should have been the first.

1.Double check the extent of the problem.

2. Ascertain if there is a dollar amount to fix the problem.

3. Check with previous owners.

4. Go over the problems with the seller.

5. Do a soft renegotiation.

6. If that fails, "take a way."

7. Consider legal action.

8. Move on.

Double check the Extent of the Problem

All older properties will have something that gives away their age. Even the best maintained property has something that may need fixing, painting, or simple repair. Aesthetic elements are simply a matter of opinion. Are you going to paint the building another color anyway? Are you planning on replacing all the AC units next year when you redo the roof? These are elements you may have already taken into consideration when you made your offer. If so, either attempt to improve the deal or move forward. But real problems that you didn't expect need to be rechecked and dealt with.I suggest the following

Ascertain If There Is a Dollar Amount to Fix the Problem

Most problems will have a dollar amount attached to them. The catch is that the final dollar amount may not be known until the job is actually finished. What looks like a simple job to replace some rotten wood might turn out to be a complete roof removal and a full roof replacement. Many residential purchase contracts have a provision for repairs. It is not uncommon for the seller to agree to a buffer of 2 percent of the purchase price to cover needed repairs. In commercial transactions in the multimillions of dollars, that might seem like a lot of money, but repairs can be very expensive.

You need to find the problem, then find out what it will cost to remedy it. Keep in mind the time it will take to make those repairs, too. On whose clock does the repair fall? If you are the buyer and don't mind being shut down for a couple of months following the closing, then let it be on your clock.

Check with Previous Owners

If the previous owners (prior to the owner you have a contract with) are still around and the time period between ownership was relatively short (two to three years), you might call or have your broker call them and discuss the current problem. If it turns out that the problem was around when they owned the property and a settlement was made when they sold it to cover its remedy, but the current owner did nothing to fix the problem, then you know what kind of seller you are dealing with. This might do nothing for you in the end, but you will have an issue to pick with the owner and a good reason to ask that the problem get fixed prior to your closing on the property.

Go over the Problems with the Seller

If the past owners give no hint at the problem or its existence in the past, then sit down with the seller and discuss the situation. Ask questions like "Did you know about this problem? Have you priced out the cost to fix it? Has any tenant complained about this problem? (If the problem has been around for a long time, then the tenant may have put the seller on notice, and this is something you might find out.) If so, what did you do about those complaints?" All this puts the seller in the "is there going to be legal action" mode, and this will either loosen the seller up for a realistic remedy, or cause the seller to simply clam up altogether and refuse to meet with you in the future. Either way, you are moving in a positive direction to decide either to buy or to walk away.

Do a Soft Renegotiation

Attempt to reconcile the deal. This is best done through your broker or lawyer. Simply send over a contract modification agreement that states that a problem exists and that the seller will agree to

(1) fix the problem to certain specifications that you spell out, or

(2) reduce the down payment or price or both by an amount of money that is either shown in the agreement or follows a formula or is based on a firm estimate from a bonded contractor. You can add to this other provisions, too, as you see fit, and then present it.

It is a good idea to do this well within the due diligence period so that you have time to attempt this and any other renegotiations, rather than running out of time and having to either go hard or walk away from the deal.

If that Fails, Take a Way

The take-a-way is a contract negotiation tactic. It works best when it occurs within the due diligence period because of its finality. Here is how it works. You have tried to do everything possible to remedy the problem or to bring the price to a level where you can satisfactorily accept the property as it is. But there is still a gap of value or time or both that you need to obtain out of the deal. So your lawyer writes a letter to the seller or the seller's lawyer that says something like this: ". . . which describes the problems that have been uncovered in the present due diligence that my client has undertaken. I have been asked to propose a drop in the price by $250,000 and an extension on the closing for another 90 days from the contract date of two months from now. Based on the current findings my client has informed me that unless the remedy which this letter proposes is acceptable to you then my client may be forced to withdraw from this agreement as the contract allows."

This does not say you will withdraw, it only hints that you might. If the seller is motivated and there are no other buyers in the wings waiting for you to drop out of the picture, this sometimes works.

Consider Legal Action

The subject of legal action might be the next step. Assume that your lawyer tried the take-a-way and there was no response. (That would likely be my reaction as a seller.) Bring the negotiations right up to the brink, but always leave a reasonable time for a decision to be made (not "I need to know within two hours"). Or, if there was a response that you don't like, then your lawyer can move to the next step:

"My client has asked me to make one more attempt to resolve this matter prior to his review of what legal actions he must take in court. If you have any thoughts about how we can solve this problem, please call me or have your lawyer give me a call so we can discuss how to bring about a speedy closing. My client has informed me that if the terms of the modification are agreeable he will increase his deposit by $500,000 and close within 30 days."

You can see that this letter hints at a potential legal action, and then goes on to hold out a carrot for a larger deposit and a quick closing if the matter is resolved right away. It is always good to make your last or even next to last overture with some positive benefit that is not in the contract.

Move On

If you cannot become satisfied with the situation and your lawyer says you don't have much of a case to go to court over, or you just don't want to deal with that issue in that way, then move on. There is always another property to buy, and as long as you have not fallen in love with the property, the breakup will be next to painless.

Move on.

If you cannot become satisfied with the situation and your lawyer says you don't have much of a case to go to court over, or you just don't want to deal with that issue in that way, then move on. There is always another property to buy, and as long as you have not fallen in love with the property, the breakup will be next to painless. Move on.

Conclusion

I will presume that by now you have successfully read this book. This means that you are properly armed to tackle commercial real estate. Income realty investments are out there waiting for you to come along. But do not think that this is going to be as easy as falling off a log. You will have to put in time and make the contacts that will ultimately be your source of knowledge that will lead you to profits. Continue to expand that knowledge at every opportunity. Never think your learning is finished. Your brain is far from empty, but there is lots of room to go.

Good luck.

www.ingramcontent.com/pod-product-compliance
Lightning Source LLC
Chambersburg PA
CBHW071456220526
45472CB00003B/821